MW00882663

CDL Study Guide
2024-2025
Edition

Ultimate Preparation Book with
Questions and Detailed Answers to
Pass the CDL Exam on Your First
Attempt

Table of contents:

Introduction 3

Chapter 1: An Overview 6

Chapter 2: Study Tips and Tricks 28

Chapter 3: Your Vehicle Safety 34

Chapter 4: Hazardous Materials (H)
Endorsement...62

Chapter 5: Tank Vehicle (N) Endorsement 75

Chapter 6: School Bus (S) Endorsement.........85

Chapter 7: Air Brakes 102

Chapter 8: Vehicle Inspection 117

Chapter 9: Basic Control...........................135

Chapter 10: Practice Test 161

Conclusion...171

Introduction

Welcome to the "CDL Study Guide 2023-2024 Edition: Ultimate Preparation Book with Questions and Detailed Answers to Pass the CDL Exam on Your First Attempt". This book is designed to be your comprehensive guide to successfully navigating the Commercial Driver's License (CDL) exam. Whether you're a novice driver just starting out or an experienced professional looking to renew your license, this guide is tailored to meet your needs.

In Chapter 1, we provide an overview of the CDL exam, breaking down its structure and what you can expect. We'll delve into the different sections of the test, the types of questions you'll encounter, and the scoring system. This chapter will equip you with a clear understanding of the exam's layout, helping you to approach your study with a strategic mindset.

Chapter 2 is all about study tips and tricks. We understand that preparing for an exam can be daunting, and we're here to help you streamline your study process. This chapter offers practical advice on how to organize your study time, techniques for retaining information, and strategies for tackling different types of questions.

In Chapter 3, we focus on vehicle safety, a critical aspect of the CDL exam. We'll cover everything from basic vehicle maintenance to emergency procedures, ensuring you're well-prepared to handle any situation that may arise on the road.

Chapter 4 delves into the Hazardous Materials (H) Endorsement. This section is crucial for drivers who will be transporting hazardous materials. We'll provide detailed explanations of the regulations and safety procedures associated with this endorsement, along with practice questions to test your understanding.

In Chapter 5, we explore the Tank Vehicle (N) Endorsement, providing in-depth coverage of the knowledge and skills required for safely operating tank vehicles.

Chapter 6 covers the school Bus (S) Endorsement. This chapter is designed for those aspiring to drive school buses, focusing on the unique safety considerations and regulations associated with this role.

In Chapter 7, we delve into the intricacies of air brakes, a common feature in commercial vehicles. We'll cover their operation, maintenance, and the potential issues that can arise, equipping you with the knowledge to handle these systems confidently.

Chapter 8 focuses on vehicle inspection, a critical skill for any commercial driver. We'll guide you through the inspection process, highlighting the key areas to focus on and common issues to watch out for.

Chapter 9, Basic Control, covers the fundamental skills required to operate a commercial vehicle. From steering and shifting to backing and parking, we'll provide detailed explanations and practical tips to help you master these skills.

Finally, in Chapter 10, we provide a comprehensive practice test. This test is designed to mimic the actual CDL exam, allowing you to gauge your readiness and identify areas where you may need further study.

Chapter 1: An Overview

The Commercial Driver's License (CDL) is a crucial prerequisite for those aspiring to drive large motor vehicles such as 18-wheelers, school or tour buses, tankers, and vehicles transporting hazardous materials. To acquire this license, one must pass stringent written and practical driving tests.

While the federal government sets the regulations for issuing the CDL, the actual tests are conducted by individual states. The concept of this license is relatively recent in the history of transportation, having been introduced in 1986 with the enactment of the Vehicle Motor and Safety Act. Before this, each state had its own rules for heavy motor vehicles, leading to confusion, unnecessary accidents, and even traffic-related fatalities.

There are three categories of CDL, labeled as A, B, and C. Each category has its own specific prerequisites. To fulfill your ambition of driving a commercial vehicle, you must satisfy at least one of these category requirements.

Class A Commercial Driver's License (CDL)

To drive a vehicle with a gross weight rating of 26,001 pounds or more, or to tow a vehicle weighing over 10,000 pounds, a Class A CDL is required. This license permits you to operate the following types of vehicles:

• Flatbed trucks

- Livestock transport vehicles

- Various types of tractor trailers (including refrigerated, dry van, tanker, and double and triple combinations)

- Tractor-trailer buses

- Truck-trailer combinations

Class B Commercial Driver's License (CDL)

A Class B CDL is necessary for operating a vehicle with a combined weight of up to 26,000 pounds or towing a vehicle weighing up to 10,000 pounds. This license allows you to drive the following types of vehicles:

- Box trucks

- Dump trucks with small trailers

- Large passenger buses

- Segmented buses

- Straight trucks

- Tractor-trailers

Class C Commercial Driver's License (CDL)

A Class C CDL is required when you need to operate a vehicle designed to transport 16 or more passengers, including the driver. This license is also necessary when your vehicle is transporting hazardous materials or any substances legally classified as dangerous. With this license, you can operate the following types of vehicles:

- Combination vehicles not covered under Class A or B licenses

- Passenger vans

- Small vehicles carrying hazardous materials (HazMat)

Commercial Driver's License (CDL) Permit

To acquire a Commercial Driver's License (CDL), the process is quite similar to obtaining a regular driving license. Firstly, you must successfully pass a general knowledge examination conducted by your state's department of motor vehicles. Once you pass, you will receive a temporary permit that only allows you to drive under the supervision of a licensed CDL holder.

CDL Endorsements

CDL endorsements are specialized certifications that demonstrate your ability to safely operate specific types of vehicles or carry certain types of loads. To earn an endorsement, you must pass a written test in the relevant area.

You can earn up to six different endorsements, which include:

1. N Tank Vehicle Endorsement

Often referred to as the tanker endorsement, this certification allows Class A and B CDL holders to operate a vehicle with a temporary or permanent tank attached. Typically, these vehicles transport liquids such as water, milk, gas, or chemicals. However, they can also carry dry loads like grain or sand.

2. H Hazardous Materials Endorsement

Also known as HazMat, this endorsement requires more time to obtain due to the risky nature of the materials transported. It is crucial for anyone transporting hazardous materials like dangerous chemicals, gas, and oil. Class A or B CDL holders are eligible for this endorsement.

3. X Tanker/HazMat Combination Endorsement

This endorsement allows Class A and B CDL holders to transport HazMat cargo using a tanker truck. The X endorsement combines both the N and H endorsements, and can be obtained through a single test.

4. T Doubles/Triples Endorsement

This endorsement, often referred to as "doubles and triples," is exclusively available to Class A CDL holders. It allows drivers to haul more than one trailer simultaneously. However, not all states permit this type of vehicle.

5. P Passenger Transport Endorsement

This endorsement is available to all CDL holders and authorizes them to operate a vehicle carrying passengers. The maximum number of passengers permitted is determined by each state.

6. S School Bus Endorsement

This endorsement allows all CDL holders to drive a school bus. However, before obtaining this endorsement, the driver must first have the P endorsement, which permits passenger transport.

How can you acquire a Commercial Driver's License (CDL)?

To be eligible for a CDL, you need to be at least 18 years old. However, this only permits you to operate within the state that issued your license. To drive interstate or across different states, you must be at least 21 years old.

The government mandates that you should be proficient in English, in terms of speaking, reading, and writing. Furthermore, you should have held a valid driver's license for a minimum of two years. You will also be required to undergo a medical examination and drug testing.

The Medical Examination

The Department of Transportation (DOT) necessitates a pre-employment medical examination, which must be conducted by a DOT-approved physician. You should provide a comprehensive list of all your medications, including dosage and frequency, along with the names and addresses of the prescribing doctors.

If you have any of the following medical conditions, it's advisable to bring all relevant documentation:

Vision: Bring your eyeglasses or contact lenses.

Hearing: Bring your hearing aid.

Diabetes: Bring your most recent Hemoglobin A1C (HgAIC) lab results and blood sugar logs.

Heart: Bring a letter from your cardiologist detailing your medical history, current medications, and a certificate of fitness to drive.

The Exam Components

The medical examination comprises five sections:

1. Vision: To qualify for a CDL, your vision should be at least 20/40 in each eye, with or without corrective lenses. You should also have a 70-inch peripheral vision in the horizontal meridian in each eye.

2. Hearing: You should be able to perceive a "forced whisper" from at least five feet away, with or without a hearing aid. This is equivalent to an average hearing loss in the better ear of less than 40 decibels.

3. Blood Pressure/Pulse Rate: Your blood pressure and pulse will be checked for hypertension and irregular heart rhythms.

4. Urinalysis: This test is conducted to detect any underlying medical conditions, such as diabetes.

5. Physical Examination: This comprehensive check-up covers twelve areas:

General appearance

Eyes: To detect signs of cataracts, glaucoma, or other eye diseases.

Ears: To check for scarring of the tympanic membrane or perforation of the eardrum.

Mouth and Throat: To identify any problems with swallowing or breathing.

Heart: To detect murmurs or the presence of a pacemaker.

Lungs and Chest: To check for abnormal breathing, low respiratory functions, and cyanosis.

Abdomen and Viscera: To identify an enlarged liver, viscera, or muscle weakness.

Vascular System: To check for abnormal pulse, carotid, or varicose veins.

Genito-Urinary: To detect hernias.

Extremities: To identify impaired limbs.

Spine: To check for previous surgeries or limitation of range of motion.

Neurological: To detect impaired equilibrium, coordination of speech pattern, ataxia, and asymmetric deep tendon reflexes.

Commercial Learner's Permit (CLP) Test

In most jurisdictions, it's mandatory to pass your medical examination before you can proceed to take the written test for your Commercial Learner's Permit (CLP). Although the process may differ from state to state, all states mandate the completion of the CLP test in the following areas:

- General knowledge

- Combination vehicle

- Air brakes

This is where our guide comes into play. While we can't assist you in passing your physical exam, we can certainly help you prepare for the written test.

Before proceeding further, it's crucial to contemplate if a career in driving—whether it's long-haul, school, or tour bus—is the right fit for you. Let me assure you, it can be an incredibly fulfilling career for the right individual.

Once you've made up your mind, it's time to hit the books. An exciting and rewarding journey awaits you.

Why Should I Obtain a Commercial Driver's License (CDL)?

A CDL can broaden your career prospects. If you're interested in professional driving, the ability to handle heavy-duty vehicles can make you more desirable to companies seeking drivers.

Indeed, there's a wealth of knowledge to acquire, numerous regulations to comprehend, and a series of classes and tests to undertake over a span of three to seven weeks to secure your license. However, many commercial drivers have managed to recover these costs in a short time and have found work environments and colleagues that are perfect for them.

Driving commercial motor vehicles may not be suitable for everyone, but for many, it's the ideal job. Travel is a given for long-haul drivers, and life on the road has its perks. The community is vibrant and thriving.

A CDL can also be beneficial for local driving jobs if you're not interested in long-haul routes. There are positions available for local pickup and delivery drivers, local routes, and even jobs that require maneuvering large machinery within specific locations like hubs or warehouses.

Possessing a CDL qualifies you for a wide array of jobs across numerous regions, states, counties, areas, and routes throughout the entire nation, and even into Canada.

Essential Competencies for Commercial Driving

While a significant portion of a commercial driver's time is spent on the road, driving proficiency isn't the sole determinant of success in this field. Other vital skills include vehicle maintenance, organization, and the ability to safely operate the vehicle under varying weather conditions.

Driving Proficiency - Mastering the art of reversing your vehicle is one of the most critical driving skills, requiring extensive practice. Inadequate reversing skills can lead to challenges in unloading or delivering cargo. Therefore, it's advisable to invest time in honing this skill to become adept at maneuvering your vehicle. As a safety measure, always exit the vehicle before reversing to avoid any potential damage.

Interpersonal Skills - Although most of your professional time will be spent in solitude on the road, effective interpersonal skills are crucial for interacting with other drivers, shippers, inspection officials, and others. It's essential to maintain a polite demeanor, even when dealing with difficult shippers, as rudeness can exacerbate the situation. Courtesy is a key attribute in this profession and should be extended to all, including your dispatcher, who can be a valuable ally during your trips. Strong interpersonal skills can significantly enhance your chances of a successful driving career.

Organizational and Cleanliness Skills - In this profession, your truck essentially serves as your office. Maintaining a clean truck signals to inspectors that you take pride in your living conditions, and you are diligent about keeping your vehicle information and paperwork organized and up-to-date. Regular cleaning routines can help maintain a pristine vehicle, making your driving experience more enjoyable. Useful tips for maintaining cleanliness include using floor mats, keeping cleaning supplies within reach, regularly sweeping your truck with a small dust broom, using an air purifier, washing the vehicle floor with soap and water, and investing in a small vacuum cleaner.

Vehicle Maintenance Skills - While you don't need to be a truck mechanic to thrive in this industry, understanding basic vehicle maintenance can simplify your job. Equipping your vehicle with a comprehensive set of repair tools enables you to perform basic repairs when necessary, helping you avoid any Department of Transportation (DOT) violations during inspections. However, it's important to remember that any major vehicle repairs should be entrusted to a qualified professional with the requisite skills, experience, and tools.

Certifications

Different types of certifications are required for each category of commercial driver's license, depending on the specific vehicle and its intended use. These certifications are issued by the federal government via the state licensing authority where you can acquire your CDL. You can secure these certifications from your state's licensing agency by successfully completing the relevant tests. Some of these tests are written, while others involve practical driving assessments. They are issued for various purposes, which I will outline below.

A - This certification is acquired when you obtain your Class A CDL and is a prerequisite for another one of these certifications.

H - Hazardous Materials Certification - This certification permits the licensed driver to transport hazardous materials. It can be obtained through a written test and a background check conducted by the Transportation Security Administration.

N - Tank Vehicle Certification - This certification permits the licensed driver to operate a tank truck. It can be obtained by passing a written test.

P - Passenger Transport Certification - This certification permits the licensed driver to operate passenger vehicles. It can be obtained by passing both a written and a driving test.

S - School Bus/Passenger Transport Combo Certification - This certification permits the licensed driver to operate school buses. To obtain this certification, you must pass a written and a driving test, as well as a background check and a sex offender registry check. This certification requires the P certification as a prerequisite.

T - Double/Triples Certification - This certification permits the licensed driver to operate double or triple semi-trailers. It can be obtained by passing a written test. Please note that some states, such as Florida, California, and New York, have banned the use of triple trailers. Always consider your state's requirements and laws when seeking licensing.

X - Tanker/HAZMAT Combo Certification - This certification permits the licensed driver to operate a combination of tank vehicles and hazardous materials. To obtain this certification, you must pass a written test.

Limitations

Similar to endorsements, Commercial Driver's Licenses (CDLs) come with certain limitations, indicated by specific letters. These letters provide a quick reference for officials to understand what the license permits and prohibits. Here's what each letter signifies:

E - Excludes Manual Transmission - This implies that the driver is not certified to operate manual transmission vehicles, which is acceptable as many commercial vehicles are automatic.

L - Excludes Full Air Brake - If a driver fails the air brake component of the test, they can still get their license with this limitation. It allows them to operate commercial vehicles that do not have an air brake system, like certain buses.

M - Restricts to Class B, C Vehicles and School Buses - Under specific circumstances, a driver can hold a Class A CDL but be authorized to operate only Class B and C vehicles.

N - Restricts to Class C Vehicles - If a driver holds a Class B CDL but their endorsement is under Class C, they are only allowed to operate Class C vehicles or school buses.

O - Excludes Operation of Class A Vehicle with a Fifth Wheel Connection - Operating a vehicle with a fifth wheel connection requires additional knowledge. This restriction means the driver is not required to operate such vehicles.

V - Variance - This limitation is added to a CDL to inform first responders and medical professionals that the driver has a medical condition that may need special attention.

Z - Excludes Operation of Commercial Vehicles with Full Air Brakes - This restriction is added if the driver's test was taken in a vehicle with hydraulic brakes.

Enhanced Commercial Privilege Guidelines

Regardless of the location where you operate your motor vehicle, specific federal and state regulations apply to your licensing and employment. These regulations are known as commercial privilege guidelines. They include:

1.   Driving a commercial motor vehicle without a Commercial Driver's License (CDL) or Commercial Learner's Permit (CLP) is prohibited. Violation of this rule may result in imprisonment or a fine ranging from $75 to $300.

2.   You are allowed to possess only one license, ideally from your home state. Violation of this rule may lead to fines, imprisonment, and the suspension of your home state license, with any additional licenses being returned.

3.   If you receive a hazardous materials endorsement, you must report and relinquish this endorsement to your CDL-issuing state within 24 hours under certain conditions. These include renouncing

your citizenship, not being a lawful permanent resident, being involuntarily committed to a mental health institution, having a conviction for certain felonies, or being wanted or indicted for some felonies.

4.   A unified computerized system exists that shares information about all CDL and CLP drivers across all states. Your driving records on this system will be verified to ensure that you do not possess more than one CLP and CDL.

5.   Each time you operate a commercial motor vehicle, you must properly fasten your seatbelt. The seatbelt is designed to secure you behind the wheel in the event of a crash, improve vehicle control, and minimize the risk of death or severe injuries. Without a seatbelt, a driver is four times more likely to suffer critical injuries if ejected from the vehicle.

6.   When applying for a commercial driving job, you must provide your prospective employer with information on all your previous driving jobs over the past 10 years.

7.   Regardless of the type of vehicle you were driving, you must inform your employer of any traffic violations within 30 days of your conviction, excluding parking violations.

8.   If your license gets canceled, suspended, revoked, or you receive a disqualification, you must notify your employer.

9.   Your employer has the right to prevent you from driving a commercial motor vehicle if your CLP or CDL is canceled or revoked, or if you possess more than one license.

Essential Guidelines for Every Truck Driver

Seek Clarification. If there's anything you're unsure about, don't hesitate to ask. It's crucial to understand details about your route, vehicle, cargo, parking spaces, and the regions you'll be traversing. Your company should have someone available to assist you, and there are numerous online resources where you can find answers from those who have had similar experiences.

Bypass Traffic When Feasible. Traffic can cause significant problems for long-distance travel. If you can avoid being stuck in traffic with numerous other drivers, it would be advantageous to do so within your planned route.

Maintain Constant Awareness of Your Trailer. Your trailer is your responsibility during transit. Stay vigilant at all times to detect any changes in its securement, ensure it's not moving improperly, and be aware of any alterations to your trailer as soon as they occur, not hours later.

Change Lanes Only When Necessary. As previously discussed, frequent lane changes can create problems for you and other road users. If you can maintain a single lane for extended distances, it's advisable to do so to maintain a consistent speed, pace, and direction, preventing any potential issues for yourself or other drivers.

Exercise Caution with Cruise Control. While a vehicle's cruise control feature can reduce the need for constant acceleration, it's recommended not to use it in adverse conditions such as icy or wet roads, or in areas requiring frequent speed adjustments like winding roads and urban areas, as it can pose a risk.

Avoid Swerving for Animals on the Road. Encountering animals on the road is not unusual for truck drivers. When this happens, remember that your commercial vehicle, weighing several thousand pounds, cannot be easily maneuvered within a short distance. Sudden swerving could destabilize your vehicle and potentially collide with other drivers. In such situations, it's best to firmly grip the steering wheel to maintain control upon impact and decelerate as much as possible before reaching the animal. Adhere to laws and regulations regarding roadkill before continuing your journey.

Stay Hydrated. Dehydration can lead to numerous unpleasant side effects. Given the air pressure difference in the cab over extended hours, it's important to drink plenty of water throughout your journey. If you're concerned about frequent stops, aim to drink 8 ounces of water every 15 minutes. Your body absorbs water at roughly this rate, so if you're not consuming 16 ounces within a 15-minute span, you should be able to hydrate adequately without unnecessary stops.

Exercise Caution During Harsh Weather. During adverse weather conditions, road safety can become a significant concern for you and other drivers. Maintain a steady pace, stay focused on the road ahead, keep a firm grip on the steering wheel, and reduce your speed if necessary. Prioritize your safety and don't succumb to the pressure of driving faster than you're comfortable with.

Ensure Adequate Rest. Fatigue and sleep deprivation can pose serious risks while driving. Lack of sleep can lead to hallucinations, delirium, or headaches over time. Make sure to take sufficient sleep breaks and prepare for your journey by resting well a week prior. Starting a trip already tired from an irregular sleep schedule can make it even more challenging to stay alert during your journey.

Maintain a Healthy and Balanced Diet. Choosing to prepare your own meals rather than buying them can save you money and safeguard your health. Using a slow cooker or crockpot allows you to control the ingredients in your meals. Start each day with a nutritious breakfast to keep you satiated throughout the day and opt for lighter meals for lunch and dinner. Limit your soda intake as it can lead to weight gain and increased hunger. If you can't eliminate soda entirely, try to reduce your daily consumption.

Adhere to Posted Speed Limits. Speed limits are prominently displayed on roads and highways to guide you on the maximum speed permissible. Adhering to these limits will help you navigate the roads and their bends safely.

Check Delivery Locations Personally. Many truck drivers overlook this, but inspecting your delivery locations can save you future trouble. When delivering cargo, particularly to a new client, find a secure parking spot, leave your vehicle for a few minutes, and survey the area. Despite assurances from shippers about regular truck deliveries, an unsuitable docking facility can cause delivery issues and potentially trap your truck. Taking a few extra minutes to assess the area can help you anticipate obstacles like ditches, posts, or low fire hydrants. Most truck accidents occur while reversing, but having a mental image of the area can help you avoid hazards.

Always Keep Survival Tools Accessible. As a truck driver, you'll spend over 57% of your time on the road, which can lead to unexpected situations. Having a set of survival tools in your truck prepares you for minor issues that may arise. Essential items include a spare tire, blanket, rescue tool, jumper cables, multi-tool knife, fire extinguisher, tire iron and jack, as well as extra food, drinks, and clothing.

Store Salt in Your Truck for Icy Conditions. If you encounter icy roads, you may find yourself stuck. Ice can reduce your tires' traction, but having salt in your truck can help you regain control faster than waiting for the ice to melt naturally.

Maintain Sufficient Space Ahead of Your Vehicle. Despite the temptation for other drivers to fill the space in front of your vehicle, it's crucial to ensure you have enough room. The primary reason is to provide ample time to stop without colliding with the vehicle ahead.

Inspect Your Truck After Parking. Reviewing your parking job can help improve your skills over time and allow you to adjust your parking to accommodate both your needs and those of others wishing to park in the same area.

Be Mindful of Your Tire Trajectory When Parking. Observing the trajectory of your tires can enhance your understanding and control of your vehicle over time. You can estimate the path of your tires when reversing into a parking space and then use the G.O.A.L. (Get Out And Look) method to confirm your predictions.

Prepare in Advance. Always carry any items you might need during your journey. It's better to have something and not need it, than to need it and not have it, especially when you're stranded on a roadside in the middle of the night. Pack all essentials, including first aid kits, emergency signaling equipment, appropriate clothing, personal hygiene products, and anything else you might need.

Invest in a Pair of Sunglasses. Sunlight reflecting off vehicles, buildings, and snow, or blinding glare from a low sun can be dangerous. Sunglasses with polarized lenses can significantly reduce glare-induced accidents. Choose sunglasses with thin frames for clear peripheral vision and curved lenses for front and side protection.

Illuminate Dock Lines When Reversing at Night. Docks can be poorly lit for night deliveries. In such situations, placing a flashlight on the dock lines can provide a focal point when reversing, saving you time and hassle.

Monitor Weather Conditions. Stay updated on weather conditions before and during your trip. By keeping track of the outside temperature, you can prepare for any changes in road conditions. This is a crucial part of trip planning and can help you take necessary precautions and prepare for adverse weather conditions.

Take Regular Breaks and Inspect Your Truck and Load. Take breaks every few hours or every 150 miles to check your load, inspect your truck, and ensure you have everything you need to continue your journey comfortably and safely.

Maintain Good Visibility. Always keep your clearance lights and headlights clean and switched on when driving. Good visibility is key to ensuring your safety. It allows other motorists to spot your vehicle and react to potential hazards more quickly.

Stay Alert and Patient. Avoid rushing and stay attentive to your surroundings. Maintaining focus on the road can be challenging over long distances and extended periods, but it's crucial for safety. If you need to refocus, take a break.

Utilize a GPS. A GPS (Global Positioning System) is an invaluable tool for those in the freight and logistics industry. It can provide real-time information about your location, route, and potential road obstructions. In case of emergencies, a GPS can guide you to safe pull-off spots, help others locate you, or direct you to nearby assistance.

Dress Comfortably. Opt for practical, comfortable clothing to reduce stress during your trip. Comfortable jeans, practical t-shirts, a hat, and comfortable driving shoes can enhance your comfort, especially on long journeys.

Exercise Extra Caution When Driving at Night. Night driving can be challenging due to altered visuals, unpredictable driver behavior, and potential fatigue. Stay alert and aware when driving at night.

Purchase From Reputable Brands. While it's tempting to save money, buying cheaper, lower-quality items can cost more in the long run. When shopping for items like exhausts, batteries, tires, LED and marker lights, aim to get the best deal from a trusted brand. Avoid unknown brands offering suspiciously low prices.

Don't Hesitate to Ask for Help. You're not expected to handle everything alone. If you need assistance or additional information, don't hesitate to ask. If immediate help isn't available, consider seeking advice online from other truckers and drivers nationwide.

Driving a commercial vehicle involves more than just operating the vehicle. You're responsible for ensuring your vehicle is roadworthy and your driving doesn't endanger other motorists. Vehicle safety is a fundamental aspect of obtaining your CDL license and must be taken seriously, as larger vehicles require extra caution. The following chapter discusses safe driving practices, including how to inspect your vehicle before, during, and after a trip.

Chapter 2: Study Tips and Tricks

The reality is that standardized tests can be a daunting challenge for some individuals. If you're among those who find these tests intimidating (which is true for most of us), there are measures you can adopt to mitigate the anxiety and ensure your success in the general knowledge examination and any endorsement tests.

This involves a dual strategy that has proven beneficial for numerous drivers. The first aspect focuses on study techniques, while the second addresses test-taking strategies. We'll discuss both these aspects in this chapter.

Study Tips

Preparing for the CDL general examination can be a daunting task. The standard state CDL manual comprises approximately 180 pages, which is a substantial amount of information to absorb. While it's crucial to familiarize yourself with the content, you'll need to devise a strategy to master the material effectively.

The saying "study smarter, not harder" has never been more relevant. If you aim to excel in the 50-question CDL general exam, you'll need to prepare well in advance. Here are five tips that have assisted me and numerous other drivers over the years:

1. Plan ahead

The CDL general knowledge test isn't something you can cram for the night before. Avoid attempting to study all night. Even if you manage to retain what you've read, the lack of sleep will likely impair your performance.

2. Identify your strengths and weaknesses

To apply for a CDL, you must have some driving experience. Most states require at least two years of driving experience. This implies that you're familiar with the basic traffic rules.

When you review your state's CDL manual, don't spend too much time on topics you already understand. After reviewing the manual, take a preliminary general knowledge test to identify your strengths and weaknesses. You might find that you're not as proficient in some areas as you thought. Identifying the areas, you need to focus on will help you develop an effective study plan. You might want to list your weak areas and allocate specific study time to each.

3. Compile your study materials

Spend some time gathering all the materials you'll need for your study sessions. This way, you won't have to interrupt your study time to look up uncertain facts. This will save you time and help maintain your focus.

4. Establish a study schedule

It's crucial to designate a specific time and place for studying. This will facilitate uninterrupted, continuous study sessions. Moreover, knowing when and how long you'll study will prepare you mentally for learning. If you live with family or roommates, ensure they understand that this is your study time.

The key to an effective study schedule is flexibility. If your chosen time and place aren't working, change them. Adjust your schedule as often as necessary to make it work for you.

5. Regularly test yourself

Don't hesitate to take practice tests as you study, including those in this book and others. These tests not only provide the correct answers but also explain them. This is a valuable learning tool. At this stage, don't be discouraged if the test indicates that you've failed. The purpose of taking these tests is to learn from your mistakes. Feel free to take these tests as often as you like. There's no penalty for doing so.

There's no rule that says you must keep your CDL manual closed when taking practice tests. Consider these practice tests as open-book tests. This is another effective learning strategy.

Strategies for Successful Exam-Taking

Feeling anxious on the day of an exam is a common experience, but it's crucial not to let this anxiety overwhelm you. Often, individuals encounter a question they can't answer and let this uncertainty affect their performance on the rest of the test. Here are some effective strategies that have proven beneficial to me.

1. Thoroughly read the question and all answer options

This might seem like an obvious piece of advice, but it's surprising how many people skim through a question, mistakenly assuming they understand what it's asking. Similarly, it's essential to read all the answer options carefully and understand their implications. You might come across answers that seem correct at first glance but aren't upon closer examination. Pay close attention to the wording.

2. Avoid making hasty decisions

This advice is closely related to the first point. Test creators often include a "plausible" answer among the choices to mislead you. This misleading option is frequently the first choice. If you hastily assume this option is correct, you might overlook the "best" answer further down. Sometimes, all the answers might seem correct, even when "all of the above" isn't an option. In such cases, select the option you believe is the most accurate.

3. Have faith in your instincts

If you're unsure about a question, your initial response is usually the most accurate. Trust it. If you have time to review the test, only change your answers if you realize you've made a blatant error. Avoid second-guessing yourself during the review process.

4. Answer all the questions you're confident about first

This strategy not only boosts your confidence but also helps maintain your momentum. Otherwise, you might spend too much time on a couple of challenging questions and run out of time to answer the ones you know. Mark any question you're unsure about and revisit it at the end. As you continue with the test, look out for clues or hints to these questions in other questions.

5. Maintain a steady pace

In many regions, the general knowledge exam is timed. Even in places where it isn't, it's crucial to keep a consistent pace. You might want to do some quick calculations to estimate how much time you can spend on each section. For instance, if a section has 30 questions and you have an hour to complete it, you have an average of two minutes per question. Check the time periodically to ensure you're on track. However, if this strategy increases your anxiety, skip it. The key is to maintain a good pace.

6. Don't leave any questions unanswered

Attempt every question. There's no penalty for guessing. If you're unsure, eliminate the clearly incorrect options—most questions have at least one. Choose from the remaining options. By eliminating the wrong ones, you increase your chances of selecting the correct answer. Move on to the next question without dwelling on it.

7. Pay attention to the wording

Certain words in the question should make you skeptical. These are usually "absolute" words like "greatest," "always," "never," and "must." Correct answers are typically not worded in absolute terms. Be cautious of exceptions as well. A question containing the word "except" should prompt you to ensure you understand the question and are alert for the correct answer. You might also encounter questions asking, "which is not correct." The word "not" may or may not be emphasized to draw your attention. Reread the question if necessary.

Chapter 3: Your Vehicle Safety

Examining Your Vehicle

The primary motivation for examining your vehicle is to guarantee the safety of your vehicle, other road users, and you as the driver. It is crucial to conduct a vehicle inspection before, during, and after each journey in your commercial motor vehicle. Identifying a defect in your vehicle during an inspection can prevent issues that could lead to time and money loss, or even an accident while on the road. Apart from conducting inspections to determine if there are any issues with your vehicle, federal and state laws also mandate these inspections. All vehicles are subject to scrutiny by federal or state inspectors, and those deemed unsafe will be taken out of service until adequately repaired.

Before operating any vehicle, review the last inspection report and ensure that any identified faults have been rectified and the vehicle has been deemed roadworthy by mechanics. Any safety-related item identified in the report must be repaired by the motor carrier, and they must certify that such repairs were made or deemed unnecessary. Remember, as the driver, the responsibility of operating a safe vehicle rests on your shoulders. You should only sign the previous report if you are confident all defects have been addressed.

In the following sections, we will discuss the steps to be taken and the things to be observed when examining your vehicle.

The 7-Point CDL Pre-Trip Vehicle Examination

This examination enables you to scrutinize all parts of your vehicle to ensure they are in optimal working condition and that you are not endangering yourself or others by operating the vehicle. Besides conducting this examination before and after each trip, it is also advisable to inspect your vehicle at least once every 24 hours if your journey requires more than a day's travel. Some trips may take several days to complete, and it is crucial to ensure safe driving throughout the journey.

This examination allows the driver to scrutinize all the critical points of the vehicle and verify their functionality. Although it may add some time to your day and you may feel tempted to rush through it, these examinations can be lifesaving. They enable you to identify potential equipment failures before they occur unexpectedly on a busy highway.

Let's explore the seven points of the pre-trip vehicle examination and how to ensure they are all in optimal working condition before you embark on and return from each journey in your commercial motor vehicle.

Section One: Overview of the Vehicle

● Look over the Driver Vehicle Inspection Report (DVIR) from the most recent journey undertaken with the commercial vehicle.

● Ensure the keys are not left in the ignition.

● Evaluate the overall state of the commercial vehicle.

- Inspect for any unusual signs of damage, wear and tear, or leaks underneath the vehicle.

- If you notice anything abnormal or malfunctioning, note it down and ensure it's thoroughly rectified before setting off on your next journey.

Section Two: Under the Hood Inspection

- Verify that all fluid levels are within safe operational limits.

- Ensure there are no fluid leaks under the hood.

- Examine the alternator, water pump, compressor belts, and air conditioning system.

- Confirm all wiring is securely attached and free from cracks, frays, or breaks.

- With the vehicle's hood open, start the engine and listen.

- Ensure there are no abnormal noises such as knocking, whining, or creaking.

- Once done, close the hood.

Section Three: Inside the Cab

- Confirm that the parking brake is engaged and shift the gear to "neutral" for manual vehicles, or "park" for automatic ones.

- Verify that all the dashboard gauges and indicator lamps are functioning correctly. After starting the engine, the oil pressure should increase to its normal level. The air pressure should also rise from approximately 50 to 90 pounds per square inch (psi) within about 3 minutes. Depending on your vehicle's specifications, build the air pressure up to the governor cut-out, usually around 120 to 140 psi. Your coolant and engine oil temperatures should gradually increase to their standard operating range. Also, inspect the voltmeter and/or ammeter to ensure they are within their normal ranges.

• Test the accelerator, brake pedal, clutch pedal, and steering wheel for any looseness, unusual noise, or feedback.

• Test the functionality of the turn signals, transmission controls, horn, headlights, dimmer switch, emergency flashers, washers, and wipers.

• Adjust and clean all your mirrors as needed. Look for any obstructions such as cracks, stickers, dirt, etc., and make necessary adjustments.

• Inspect the seat belt and make any necessary adjustments to ensure it is working correctly. Look for any signs of damage like rips and frays.

• Confirm the availability and readiness of all safety and emergency equipment. Your first aid kit and fire extinguisher should be securely fastened and ready for use. Unless your vehicle has circuit breakers, you should have spare electrical fuses, along with three liquid burning flares, six fuses, or three reflective triangles. Check the expiration date on your fire extinguisher and ensure it is properly charged and rated, as well as the expiry dates of any medicines in your first aid kit. Optional items like tire-changing equipment, emergency numbers, and chains for winter conditions should also be checked.

• Check the indicator lights of your vehicle's anti-lock braking system if it is equipped with one. If functioning correctly, the light on the dashboard should flash on and then off. If the light remains on, it is likely that the ABS is malfunctioning. In trailers, if the yellow light on the left rear stays on, it indicates that the ABS is not working properly.

Section Four: Lights and Indicators

• With the parking brake engaged, turn off the engine and keep the keys with you.

• Switch on the four-way emergency flashers and low beams, then exit the vehicle. Inspect the headlights, the hazards (flashers), the running lights, and the high beams to ensure they are all functioning correctly.

Section Five: Conduct a Comprehensive Walk-Around Inspection

• Start by positioning yourself in front of the vehicle to check the functionality of the four-way flashers and ensure the low beam headlights are operational.

• Activate the dimmer switch to assess the high beam headlights. Following this, turn off the four-way emergency flashers and headlights.

• Switch on the clearance, parking, identification, and side-marker lights. Engage the right turn signal and commence the walk-around inspection. As you proceed, meticulously clean any glass, reflector, or lights that appear dirty or dusty.

Inspecting the Left Front Side of the Vehicle

• On the left front side of the vehicle, verify the proper functioning of door locks and latches. Examine the tires for any bulges, severe cuts, or wear, and confirm they are adequately inflated.

• Scrutinize the wheel and rim for indications of misalignment or any bent, broken, or missing lugs, clamps, or studs.

• Utilize a wrench to check for loose lug nuts and tighten as needed.

• Look for any hub oil leaks and ensure the oil level is satisfactory.

• Evaluate the shock absorber, shackles, spring, u-bolts, and spring hangers for any looseness or damage.

• Assess the condition of the vehicle's hoses and brake disc or drum.

Inspecting the Front of the Vehicle

• Check the condition of the front axle and steering system for any loose, damaged, missing, or bent parts. Grasp the steering wheel to test for looseness.

• The windshield should be inspected for damage and thoroughly cleaned if dirty. Check the wiper arms to confirm they have normal spring tension. Wiper blades should be securely attached, and there should be no damage or stiff rubber.

• The vehicle's reflectors and lights should be clean, operational, and always display the correct color. Identification, clearance, and parking lights, along with the reflectors, should exhibit an amber color at the front. The front right turn signal should emit either white or amber light from the vehicle's forward-facing signals.

Right Side of the Vehicle

• Repeat all checks done on the left front side on this side of the vehicle as well.

• If the vehicle is designed such that the cab is over the engine, keep both the primary and secondary safety cab locks engaged.

• The fuel tank or tanks should be adequately filled, securely mounted and inspected for any leaks or damages. Ensure that the cap(s) is on and secure along with the fuel crossover line.

RIGHT REAR

- The vehicle's rims and wheels should be inspected for any missing or damaged parts.

- The tires should also be checked to make sure the tire pressure level is adequate and that there is no damage, friction, or obstruction.

- All tires fitted on the vehicle should be of a single type and not mixed. For instance, you should not fit a bias tire and radial tire on the same vehicle.

- Look for any leaks in the wheel seals or bearing.

- Check to see if all the tires are of an even size.

SUSPENSION

- Inspect the spring hangers, spring(s), u-bolts, and shackles, and make sure the axle(s) is secure with no lubricant leaks from the powered axle(s).

- Check the condition of the shock absorber, air ride components, bushings, and torque rod arms for any damages or necessary adjustments.

- If the vehicle is equipped with a retractable axle, examine the lift mechanism thoroughly. In case it is air-powered, look out for any leaks or drips.

BRAKES

● Adjust the vehicle brakes as needed.

● Check the brake discs or drum and hoses for damage or wear from friction.

REFLECTORS AND LIGHTS

● The side-marker reflectors and lights should be clean, functional, and display the proper color when in use i.e. red at the rear and amber everywhere else.

Rear

● Make sure the vehicle's license plate or plates are present, clean, and properly secured.

● There should be damage-free splash guards that are well fastened so they do not come in contact with the ground or the vehicle's tires.

● For trucks, verify that your cargo is secure, the end gates work properly, and that they are correctly secured in appropriate stake sockets.

● The doors should be properly closed with all necessary lights and/or signs mounted correctly.

• Check to see if the reflectors, tail lights, identification, and rear clearance lights are clean and functioning, and show a proper red color at the rear. Look at the right turn signal on the rear and ensure it is working and displaying either a yellow, amber, or red color.

Left Side of the Vehicle

• Repeat a check of all items inspected on the right side of the vehicle.

• Check the vehicle's battery or batteries if it is outside the engine compartment to see if they're properly secured with the box or boxes firmly mounted to the vehicle.

• Verify that the box has a firm cover and that the battery or batteries are prevented from shifting during transit. The battery should be leak and damage-free as well.

• Except for maintenance-free batteries, confirm that the fluid is at the right level, cell caps are present and tightly fastened, and the vents in the caps don't contain any foreign material.

Condition of Visible Parts

• The engine's rear and transmission should be free of leaks, there should be no cracks or bends in the frame and cross members; and the exhaust system should be secure without leaks or direct contact with wires, air lines, or fuel lines.

- All electrical wiring and air lines should be properly secured to prevent wear, friction, or snagging.

- If equipped, check for damages to the spare tire rack or carrier and see that the tire and/or wheel is properly mounted.

- Lastly, ensure the spare is adequate for your vehicle in terms of correct size and tire pressure level.

Cargo Securement for Trucks

- The cargo should be correctly tied, blocked, chained, braced, etc. to the vehicle.

- If required, make sure the header board is secure and adequate.

- Properly secure the tarp or canvas if required so that there is no billowing or tearing, and the mirrors are not obstructed.

- Verify that the curbside compartment doors are working properly and are firmly closed or locked with the necessary security seals on them.

- If there are stakes and sideboards equipped, ensure they are strong enough to support the cargo, damage-free, and properly set.

- All required signs i.e. reflectors, lamps, and flags should be correctly and safely mounted with all needed permits in the driver's possession if the cargo is oversize.

Section Six: Inspect Signal and Brake Lights

- Enter the vehicle and ensure all lights are turned off. Then, activate your brake lights either by using your handbrake or by having someone assist with the brake pedal. Proceed to switch on the left-turn signal lights.

- Exit the vehicle and verify that the brake lights, left front turn signal light, and left rear signal light are all operational, clean, and displaying the correct color. The front-facing signal light should be white or amber, while the rear signal light should be amber, yellow, or red.

- Re-enter the vehicle and switch off any unnecessary lights that are not essential for driving.

- Ensure that you have all the necessary permits, manifests, documents, etc., required for your journey.

- Secure any loose items in the cabin as they could potentially cause harm in the event of an accident or obstruct your ability to operate the controls effectively.

Section Seven: Start Engine and Test Brakes

- Restart the engine.

● If the vehicle's brakes are hydraulic, pump the pedal three times and then firmly press and hold it for approximately five seconds. The pedal should remain stationary during this process- if it moves, it indicates a malfunction or a leak. Ensure such issues are appropriately addressed before driving the vehicle.

● Test the vehicle's parking brake by fastening your seatbelt and setting the brake. If applicable, release the brake and shift into low gear. To ensure it holds, gently pull forward against it and repeat these steps with the power unit parking brakes and trailer parking brake set released. If the brake fails to hold the vehicle, it should be repaired as soon as possible.

● To assess the vehicle's service brake stopping response, drive at about 5 mph and firmly press the brake pedal. If the pedal veers to one side or the other, it could indicate a malfunction in the brake. A delay in stopping or an unusual pedal feel could also suggest a problem.

Vehicle Inspection During a Journey

Throughout your journey, it's crucial to remain vigilant and attentive to any potential issues. Regularly monitor your vehicle's gauges and inspect key components such as brakes, coupling devices, tires, wheels, rims, reflectors, lights, cargo securement devices, and electrical and brake connections to the trailer at each stop.

Post-Journey Vehicle Inspection

After each day, trip, or duty tour, it's essential to thoroughly inspect each vehicle you drive. Typically, the post-journey inspection involves completing a vehicle condition report to document any problems or malfunctions encountered. This report is vital in keeping the motor carrier informed about the necessary repairs and their timing.

Key Points to Consider When Inspecting Your Vehicle

- Check for excessive or insufficient air pressure.

- Look for fabric showing through the sidewall or tread or other signs of significant wear.

- Detect any separation of tread.

- Inspect for cracked or cut valve stems.

- Ensure tire sizes are matched.

- Avoid retreaded, regrooved, or recapped tires on a bus's front wheels.

- Check for cut or damaged tires.

- Ensure dual tires are not touching vehicle parts or each other.

- Avoid using bias-ply and radial tires together.

- Look out for damaged rims.

- Check for missing lugs, spacers, clamps, or studs.

- Avoid rims or wheels with unsafe welding repairs.

- Inspect for bent, cracked, or mismatched lock rings.

- Rusty wheel nuts may indicate looseness.

- Check for cracked brake drums.

- Avoid oily or greasy brake shoes or pads.

- Ensure no broken, missing, or dangerously thin brake shoes.

- Check for missing cotter keys, bolts, nuts, or other steering system parts.

- Ensure less than ten degrees of steering wheel play.

- Check for broken, loose, or bent steering system parts.

- Look for leaks in vehicle fluid, pumps, and hoses for power steering systems.

- Check for spring hangers that allow improper axle placement.

- Ensure no broken or missing leaves in leaf springs.

- Look for leaky shock absorbers.

- Check for leaking and/or damaged air suspension systems.

- Inspect for broken, cracked, loose, or missing frame members.

- Check for missing, damaged, or cracked spring hangers, u-bolts, torque rod/arm, or other axle positioning parts.

- Look for shifted or broken leaves in a multi-leaf spring that can hit other vehicle parts or tires.

- Check for leaky exhaust system parts.

- Ensure no broken, missing, or loose nuts, bolts, clamps, or mounting brackets.

- Check for exhaust system parts rubbing against moving vehicle parts or fuel system parts.

- Ensure no broken, missing, or loose vertical stacks, mufflers, exhaust pipes, or tailpipes.

- Look for imbalanced or overloaded cargo.

• Ensure placarding and proper documentation for cargo containing hazardous materials.

Understanding Your Air Brakes and Their Components

Gaining knowledge about your vehicle's components can enhance your ability to operate it safely and efficiently. In this segment, we will delve into the elements of an air brake system, providing a brief overview of each part. To proficiently drive a commercial motor vehicle (CMV) equipped with air brakes, it's crucial to thoroughly comprehend the information in this section. Additionally, reviewing Chapter 7 on combination vehicles will be beneficial when operating trailers with air brakes.

To begin, an air brake is a system that utilizes compressed air to activate the braking mechanism. Air brakes are composed of three distinct systems: the service brake, parking brake, and emergency brake. The service brake system is used during regular driving and is responsible for applying and releasing the brakes. The parking brake system comes into play when the vehicle's parking brake control is utilized, applying and releasing the parking brakes. The emergency brake system, on the other hand, activates certain components of the parking and service brake systems to stop the vehicle in the event of a brake system failure. While air brakes are safe and highly effective in stopping particularly heavy or large vehicles, they must be used appropriately and maintained regularly.

Air Compressor

An air compressor is an essential component of every air brake system, responsible for pumping air into the air storage tanks, also known as reservoirs. The compressor is linked to the vehicle's engine through gears or a v-belt. It may be cooled either by air or the engine's cooling system. The air compressor may derive its oil supply from an attached source or the engine oil. If your vehicle's air compressor has its own oil source, it's crucial to check it before and after each journey during your pre and post-trip inspections.

Air Compressor Governor

The air compressor governor serves as a regulator for the air compressor, determining when it pumps air into the air storage tanks. When the tank's air pressure reaches the "cut out" level or the required pressure (around 125 PSI), the governor halts the air flow. Once the pressure falls below the "cut in" level, the governor reactivates the compressor, restoring it to the cut-out level.

Air Storage Tanks

Air storage tanks, also referred to as reservoirs, store the air required for your braking system. The number of tanks your vehicle has may vary depending on its size. It's important to familiarize yourself with your vehicle's system and the number of tanks it requires. These tanks store sufficient air to enable the truck to brake multiple times, even if the air compressor fails. If an air compressor failure occurs, seek professional service as soon as possible.

Air Tank Drains

Compressed air usually contains traces of water and compressor oil, which can accumulate and potentially disrupt your brakes. The water in the air tank can freeze, potentially leading to brake failure. To prevent this, ensure you drain all your air tanks thoroughly before leaving your truck overnight. Each air tank should have a drainage valve at its base. There can be different types of drainage valves, so it's important to consult your vehicle's manuals and understand how to operate them.

A manually-operated drainage valve is typically activated by a quarter turn or a pull cable and should be used at the end of each driving day.

An automatic drainage valve self-drains the tanks, but may also have a manual mechanism in case of failure. Some air tanks can also be manually drained. Additionally, air tanks equipped with electric heating devices are available, which can prevent and reverse freezing of the automatic drain during freezing weather.

Alcohol Evaporator

An alcohol evaporator is not a standard component in all air brake systems, but it serves a critical function in those that do have it. It is designed to evaporate alcohol introduced into the air system. The alcohol helps to mitigate the risk of ice formation within the braking system during cold or inclement weather, as ice can hinder the system's proper functioning.

If your system includes an alcohol container, it's essential to check and refill it to the required levels daily during cold weather. However, this does not eliminate the need for daily draining of your air tanks. It's crucial to expel water and oil from these tanks to ensure their optimal operation. This can be done manually or through functioning automatic drain valves.

Safety Valve

Also known as a safety relief valve, this pressure release valve is positioned on the first of your air tanks filled by the compressor. It allows for the release of excess pressure before it circulates through the rest of the system. The valve is engineered to open at 150 PSI. However, if the valve does trigger and release air, it indicates a fault that needs to be rectified by a mechanic to prevent future occurrences.

Brake Pedal

The brake pedal is a familiar component to most people, especially drivers. It's the pedal you depress to activate the brakes and decelerate or halt the vehicle. The force with which you press the pedal determines the speed at which the vehicle slows down or stops. Lifting your foot off the brake releases the air brake pressure. The air compressor can replenish this air pressure, but it requires some time to do so.

Avoid unnecessary pressing and releasing of the brake, as the air compressor may struggle to maintain the rate of pressure release, potentially leading to brake failure due to insufficient pressure. When the brake pedal is depressed, a spring and the air pressure directed to the brakes generate a force against your foot. Being aware of this can help you gauge the air pressure level in the brakes.

Foundation Brakes

Foundation brakes are situated and operate adjacent to each wheel of the vehicle. These should be inspected during your pre-trip check and at regular intervals. The s-cam drum brake is the most common type. The components of the foundation brake include:

Brake Linings, Shoes, and Drums - Each axle end of your vehicle has brake drums, which house the braking mechanism for each wheel. The brake shoes and linings are pressed against the drum's interior. The friction generated during braking and its impact on your brake components depend on the intensity and duration of brake usage. Excessive heat can cause brake failure.

S-cam Brakes - Depressing the brake pedal allows air into the brake chamber. The resulting pressure extends the pushrod, moving the slack adjuster and twisting the brake camshaft. The S-shaped s-cam turns, pushing the brake shoes apart and against the drum's interior. Releasing the brake pedal returns the s-cam to its original position, moving the brake shoes away from the drum and allowing the wheels to roll freely. S-cam brakes are the most prevalent type of foundation brakes.

Wedge Brakes - These brakes function differently. The brake chamber push rod pushes a wedge between two brake shoes' ends, forcing them apart and against the drum's interior. Some wedge brakes have a single chamber, while others have two, enabling wedges to push the brakes in opposite directions. Some wedge brakes self-adjust, while others require manual adjustment.

Disc Brakes - Air-operated disc brakes also have a slack adjuster and brake chamber like s-cam brakes. However, instead of the S-shaped mechanism, disc brakes have a component called a "power screw".

The brake chamber pressure turns the power screw via the slack adjuster. The power screw clamps down on the disc or "rotor" between the brake pads on a caliper, similar to a large C-clamp.

Pressure Gauges for Air Brakes

Vehicles equipped with an air brake system have a pressure gauge attached to the air tank. For vehicles with a dual air brake system, there is either a separate gauge for each half of the system or two needles on a single gauge. These gauges indicate the amount of air pressure in the tanks.

Brake Application Pressure Gauge

Not all vehicles have this gauge, which shows the amount of pressure applied to the brakes. If you find yourself needing to apply more pressure to the brake pedal to maintain speed, it could be a sign of wear and tear on the brakes. This could also indicate brakes that are out of adjustment, air leaks, or other mechanical issues. In such cases, it's advisable to slow down and shift to a lower gear.

Low Air Pressure Warning

Legally, your vehicle must provide a visible warning if the air brake system's pressure falls below 60 psi. This warning is typically a red light, often accompanied by a buzzer. Some vehicles also have a mechanical arm, known as a "wig wag", that drops into view when the pressure is dangerously low and retracts when the pressure is restored. If the pressure remains too low, the arm will not stay retracted. For buses, this alert usually triggers at 80 to 85 PSI.

Brake Light Switch

This mechanism activates your brake lights when you apply the brakes, signaling to other drivers that you're slowing down.

Front Brake Limiting Valve

Vehicles manufactured before 1975 often have this component, which reduces the air pressure applied to the front brakes when set to "slippery". While this was designed to prevent skidding on slippery surfaces, it can also reduce the vehicle's stopping power. Therefore, it's recommended to keep the control set to "normal" for optimal braking. Some vehicles have automatic front wheel limiting valves, which reduce air to the front brakes unless the brakes are applied very hard.

Spring Brakes

Most commercial vehicles are required to have spring brakes and a parking brake. These brakes are held in place mechanically, as air pressure can leak away. The springs apply the brakes when the air pressure is removed. If all the air in the system leaks out, the brakes will engage. However, these brakes will only fully engage when the air pressure drops to between 20 and 45 psi. Therefore, it's important to stop the vehicle safely as soon as the low air pressure warning is activated. Proper adjustment of the brakes is crucial for them to function correctly.

Parking Brake Controls

Newer vehicles with air brakes usually have a yellow, diamond-shaped push-pull control knob for the parking brake. Older vehicles may have a lever instead. Regardless of the control type, the parking brake should be used whenever the vehicle is parked.

Warning: Do not press the brake pedal when the spring brakes are activated. The combined force of the air pressure and the springs could potentially harm the brakes. While many brake systems are designed with safeguards to prevent this, it is still advisable to avoid this situation as not all systems have these protections. The safest practice is to refrain from using the brake pedal when the spring brakes are in use.

Modulating Control Valves: Some vehicles are equipped with a modulating control valve, a dashboard handle that allows for gradual application of the spring brakes. This spring-loaded lever provides the driver with a sense of the braking action, enabling them to adjust the braking intensity as needed. Greater lever movement results in quicker brake engagement, offering maximum control in case of service brake failure. When parking your vehicle using the modulating control valve, push it to its maximum limit and secure it in place with the locking device.

Dual Parking Control Valves: When the main air pressure decreases, the spring brakes are activated. Certain vehicles, such as buses, have separate air tanks that can be used to disengage the spring brakes, facilitating emergency parking. One of the dashboard valves, which operates by pushing and pulling, is used to activate the spring brakes for parking. The other valve, spring-loaded in the "out" position, must be pushed in to release air from the separate tank, thereby loosening the spring brakes and allowing vehicle movement. Releasing this button reapplies the spring brakes. The air tank only holds enough pressure for a few uses, so the driver must strategize their moves to maximize usage.

Anti-Lock Braking System (ABS)

Since March 1, 1998, all commercial motor vehicles have been required to have Anti-Lock Braking Systems (ABS). This regulation was enforced on truck tractors a year earlier, from March 1, 1997. Many commercial vehicles manufactured before these dates are still equipped with ABS, so it's advisable to refer to your owner's manual to confirm the type of braking system in your vehicle. The certification label will provide the manufacturing date of your vehicle.

ABS is a computerized system designed to prevent wheel lock-up during sudden and hard braking. Vehicles with ABS usually have a yellow warning or malfunction indicator on the dashboard to alert the driver of any potential issues.

Trailers are also fitted with yellow ABS malfunction indicators, located on the left side, either at the front or rear corner. Similarly, dollies manufactured after March 1, 1998, are required to have a lamp on the left side for this purpose.

In more recent vehicle models, the ABS malfunction indicator lights up when the vehicle is started, to reassure the driver of its presence and functionality. In older models, this indicator may remain lit until the vehicle reaches a speed of at least five miles per hour.

If the indicator remains lit after a few seconds of driving, or if it lights up again after the initial bulb check, it may indicate an ABS failure in one or more wheels.

It's crucial to understand that ABS is not an add-on to your vehicle's standard braking system. It neither enhances nor reduces your regular braking ability during normal driving situations. ABS only activates when the wheels are on the verge of locking up due to abrupt braking.

When ABS is engaged, aim to maintain a long braking distance. While ABS doesn't necessarily reduce the braking distance, it does help maintain vehicle control during hard braking.

Exhaust

Exhaust system defects can be extremely hazardous as they can cause harmful fumes to leak into the cab or sleeper berth. During your pre-trip inspection, examine the exhaust for any loose, broken, missing, or leaking components. This includes exhaust pipes, mufflers, mounting brackets, bolts or nuts, clamps, and vertical stacks. Also, look out for parts that might be hitting or rubbing against the fuel system, tires, or other moving parts of the vehicle.

Inspections During Your Journey

While on your travel route, it's advisable to stop periodically to inspect your load and vehicle, ensuring that no issues have arisen on the road that could cause problems later.

This inspection won't need to be as comprehensive as the pre-trip and post-trip inspections. You should still check your tires and brakes and do a walk-around of the vehicle to ensure there are no visible issues. However, you won't need to open the hood or check for less obvious issues.

When inspecting your cargo, look for any slippage or shifting. If there's significant shifting, you might need to secure your load differently to prevent further movement during your journey.

Power Steering

Power steering is a crucial feature in all vehicles, including small personal cars. If you've ever experienced a car running out of gas or power steering fluid, you'll know how challenging it is to steer the vehicle without it. It's essential to ensure your vehicle has sufficient power steering fluid before and after any journey. This can be checked using the dipstick or sight glass, if your reservoir has one. For optimal performance, the fluid level should be well above the refill mark.

Tires

● Tires not located at the front of the vehicle should have a tread depth of no less than 2/32 of an inch, be evenly worn, and have no cuts or damage to the tread or sidewall.

● All other tires should have a tread depth of no less than 4/32 of an inch, be evenly worn, and have no cuts or damage to the tread or sidewall.

● Rims should be free of cracks or damage, with no signs of welding repair or damage.

- The axle seal should be leak-free, and if there's a sight glass, the level should be adequate.

- All lug nuts should be present, secure, and show no signs of looseness such as rust trails or shiny threads. There should be no cracked or distorted lug nuts or bolt holes.

- The hub seal should be at an adequate level and not leaking.

- Tire pressure valve stems and caps should be present and not leaking.

- Tire pressure should range from 90 to 100 psi for both the front driver's side tire and other tires. This should be confirmed by the manufacturer's manual and the state requirements for your vehicle.

Vocabulary and Keywords

ABS (Anti-Lock Braking System) - ABS is a braking assistance system used in commercial vehicles to prevent wheel lock-up and skidding when brakes are suddenly applied.

Air Brake - Air brakes utilize a pressurized air system to halt a commercial vehicle. A mandatory Air Brakes Knowledge Test must be passed to demonstrate proficiency in operating vehicles equipped with air brakes.

Axle Weight - The weight exerted on the ground by one axle or a set of axles.

Cargo - The load or freight carried by the truck and its driver.

Container – A term used for large, metal shipping containers, typically transported by rail or truck, ranging from 20 to 40 feet in length.

Coupling Device Capacity - The maximum weight that coupling devices can handle. These devices must keep vehicles connected, so it's crucial to ensure that the vehicle can bear the weight placed on it.

Dry Bulk - Unpackaged, raw materials shipped in large tanks or containers, such as grain or metal. Some companies specialize exclusively in dry bulk delivery.

Foundation Brakes - The main braking system activated when the brake pedal on the driver's side is pressed. This system is used to slow down and stop the vehicle.

GCVWR (Gross Combined Vehicle Weight Rating) - A manufacturer's specification that indicates the maximum weight that a vehicle can carry.

GCW (Gross Combination Weight) - The total weight of a vehicle, including its load, tractor, and trailer.

Governor – A device used to regulate the maximum speed of a commercial vehicle. These are used with large fleets to ensure drivers adhere to safety and legal guidelines, maximizing safety and fuel efficiency.

GVW (Gross Vehicle Weight) - The total weight of the vehicle, including the container, cargo, trailer, and tractor.

GVWR (Gross Vehicle Weight Rating) - A manufacturer's specification that indicates the maximum weight of cargo a vehicle can carry.

Suspension System - The system in the vehicle that includes components like springs, tires, shock absorbers, and linkages, allowing the vehicle to coordinate steering with the wheels for smooth handling and ride quality.

Tire Load - The maximum weight each tire on a commercial vehicle is approved to carry.

Chapter 4: Hazardous Materials (H) Endorsement

Hazardous materials, often referred to as HazMat or HM in government regulations, are substances that pose a risk to human health, safety, or property during transportation. These materials can range from gases, explosives, and flammable or combustible liquids and solids, among others. However, this list is not all-inclusive. The classification of a substance as hazardous depends on its characteristics and the shipper's interpretation of whether it meets the definition of a hazardous material.

The management of these materials is strictly regulated at all levels of government due to their inherent risks and potential repercussions. The Hazardous Materials Regulations (HMR) are outlined in Parts 100-185 of Title 49 of the Code of Federal Regulations, often referred to as 49 CFR 100-185.

Vehicles transporting hazardous materials must display a diamond-shaped, square-on-point warning sign, known as a placard.

Before applying for a hazardous materials endorsement, a background check through the Hazardous Materials Endorsement Threat Assessment Program is mandatory, whether for a new endorsement or a renewal.

Drivers intending to transport hazardous materials must undergo training and pass a written test, provided by their employer or a designated representative. Employers are legally required to keep a record of this training for all employees, even up to 90 days after an employee's departure. Furthermore, federal regulations mandate additional training and testing for those handling hazardous materials at least every three years.

The information provided here is designed to help you pass your written test, but it's important to note that this only covers a fraction of the knowledge required to safely handle hazardous materials. Reading the Federal Regulations mentioned above can provide further insights. These can be found online at the Government Printing Office bookstore and through various industry publishers.

These regulations, sometimes referred to as "contaminant regulations," are designed to ensure the safety of the driver, their loved ones, and the environment. They guide shippers on how to package these commodities and the correct procedures for loading and unloading these materials.

Shippers are required to inform drivers and other relevant parties about the risks associated with transporting these materials. This includes providing warning labels on the products, supplying the driver with necessary paperwork, including emergency response information and the required placards. The risks associated with these materials must be clearly communicated at all stages of handling to the shipper, the carrier, and the driver.

Hazardous Material Endorsement Test

The basic prerequisites for a hazardous material (HazMat) endorsement include the capability to recognize hazardous items, safely load shipments, and ensure that the vehicle is appropriately marked with the correct placards. By understanding and adhering to these regulations, you contribute significantly to minimizing the risks associated with transporting these materials.

Transportation Permits

Certain areas across the country necessitate permits for the transportation of specific explosives and large quantities of hazardous waste material. Permits might also be required for hazardous and medical waste. Additional restrictions imposed by state and county authorities may reroute your journey through designated hazardous material routes.

Transporting the Material

Inspecting your vehicle before and during each trip is always crucial, but it becomes even more critical when transporting HazMat. Law enforcement agencies have the authority to halt the vehicle, scrutinize your shipping documents, commercial driver's license (CDL), and HazMat endorsement, as well as the placards. They can also interrogate you about your knowledge regarding hazardous products.

The shipper must follow certain procedures to ensure compliance with all regulations when intending to transport a hazardous item from one location to another, whether by truck, train, ship, or airplane. They are responsible for choosing the appropriate products based on the relevant regulations. Once decided, they must ship under the hazard classification with a unique identifier and proper packaging. The packaging must include the correct labels and markers, along with the necessary placards.

The shipper's subsequent responsibilities include accurately preparing the paperwork, providing the necessary emergency response information, and supplying the carrier with the placards along with all packaging, marking, and labels.

As the carrier (or the driver), you must verify that the shipment was prepared according to the standards on the shipping document by ensuring the shipper has correctly characterized the material. It's crucial to ensure that everything is tagged, labeled, and properly prepared for shipment before you take possession of the load.

It's the driver's responsibility to reject any shipment that is not correctly prepared or identified. You're also obligated to report all accidents involving hazardous materials to the relevant government agency.

You are not required and, indeed, should reject any product that is leaking.

Once you've accepted the shipment, you must mark your vehicle according to the type of shipment and transport it in compliance with all the requirements pertaining to the specific item.

As the driver, you are also responsible for ensuring the proper storage of the material, its paperwork, and emergency response information.

Handling and Transportation of Hazardous Materials

As a carrier, it is of utmost importance that you take all necessary precautions to ensure the safety of the cargo. During loading, ensure that the cargo is kept away from any equipment that could potentially damage the container or its packaging. Hooks should not be used for loading such cargo. Maintain a distance of at least 25 feet from the material while loading.

Smoking is strictly prohibited in the vicinity of hazardous materials. Ensure that no one is smoking during the loading process. Always engage the parking brake before loading or unloading to prevent the vehicle from moving. Extra caution should be exercised in hot environments as many hazardous substances can become more dangerous when exposed to heat.

Regularly check the condition of the packaging for any leaks. Transporting hazardous materials that are leaking is strictly forbidden.

Once the material is loaded, the packaging should not be opened until it reaches the designated destination. The material should not be transferred from one shipment to another while the vehicle is in motion.

The following items should be securely packed to prevent any movement during transit:

• Gases

• Oxidizers

• Flammable solids and liquids

• Explosives

• Corrosives

• Radioactive materials

• Poisons

Safety Precautions for Handling Hazardous Materials

The following guidelines are designed to minimize risk when handling hazardous materials:

• Switch off the vehicle before loading or unloading.

• All heat sources should be turned off.

• Ensure that the floor lining is secure and not made of metallic or ferrous metal.

• Handle explosives with utmost caution. Do not throw or drop them.

• Do not transport any package that is damp or stained with oil.

• All radioactive materials should be labeled with a Yellow III.

• Class 4 and 5 materials should always be kept dry.

- Ensure adequate ventilation for combustible materials.

- Load corrosive materials one after the other and keep them upright.

- Corrosive materials should not be loaded near explosives, blasting agents, oxidizers, or poisonous gases.

- Cylinders should ideally be transported on racks. If your trailer does not have racks, ensure the floor is flat. Cylinders can be kept upright or horizontal.

- Do not store any material marked as poisonous with food or in the driver's cab.

- In case of an emergency stop along the roadside, use red lights or reflective triangles instead of flares.

Bulk Packaging and Labeling

All bulk containers, including portable and transport tanks, must be clearly marked with a hazardous identification (HID). Portable tanks should also display the owner or renter's name and the shipping name on two sides. If the tank's capacity exceeds 1,000 gallons, the shipping name should be at least two inches high. The tank's identification numbers should be visible from all sides when mounted on the vehicle. For tanks with a capacity of less than 1,000 gallons, the lettering should be one inch high.

Railroad Crossings

When transporting hazardous materials, you must come to a complete stop before crossing any railroad track. Check for trains by listening and looking in both directions. Your vehicle should be no closer than 15 feet and no further than 50 feet from the track. Only proceed to cross the tracks when it's safe, and avoid shifting gears while doing so.

Driving and Parking Regulations

Avoid parking on private property without informing the owner about the hazardous nature of your cargo. The parked vehicle should be under constant supervision unless it's parked in a designated safe haven. If your job requires you to park your placarded vehicle, you can do so within five feet of the road for a short period. Never park on a public road or shoulder without regular supervision, and don't leave a detached trailer unattended on a public road. Parking your hazardous load within 300 feet of an open fire, a bridge, a building, a tunnel, or in a crowded area is strictly prohibited.

Communication Rules

In case of an accident, it's crucial to communicate the type of hazardous material you're carrying to emergency personnel. This can minimize risk and aid in a safer response. Therefore, the following communication rules apply:

- Shippers must clearly specify the types of hazardous materials in the shipment.

- A 24/7 staffed phone number should be included in the shipping papers.

- The carrier and driver must keep the hazmat shipping papers in an easily accessible location.

- The driver should store all hazmat materials in a bag in the door pouch closest to them for easy visibility.

Emergencies

Emergency personnel like police, firefighters, and industry workers follow specific guidelines to protect the public during emergencies involving hazardous materials. These guidelines, provided by the Department of Transportation, are organized by the correct shipping name and the assigned number of the hazardous items.

In case of an accident while transporting hazardous materials, you should:

- Keep the public away from the area.

- Notify the relevant emergency personnel.

- Provide the shipment papers and response instructions to the emergency personnel.

Avoid attempting to extinguish hazardous material fires unless you're properly trained. Such fires require special training and gear. If you encounter a fire, call for help immediately.

Before exiting the vehicle, check the doors for heat. If the doors are hot, don't open them as it can fuel the fire. Often, a fire will smolder until help arrives and doesn't cause much damage.

Never attempt to contain a fire that has already started. Ensure you have the cargo documents ready to hand over to the emergency personnel.

Leaks

In the event that you detect a leak in your shipment, refer to the shipping documents, labels, or the location of the package to identify the items that are leaking. The material could potentially be hazardous to anyone who comes into contact with it.

Avoid attempting to identify the leaking material by its smell. Also, refrain from trying to pinpoint the source of the leak. Some harmful gases are undetectable by smell and could pose a risk to your health.

Hazardous Material Warning Labels

Most hazardous material packaging comes with a diamond-shaped warning label. This label is usually affixed directly to the shipment. If the label doesn't fit, it can be attached to a tag that is securely fastened to the shipment. For compressed gas cylinders, hazardous material tags are applied directly.

Terminology

The following terms are commonly used in hazardous material transportation:

Bulk packaging: This refers to hazardous materials packaged in a container that is not a vessel or a tank, without any secondary containment. Examples include transport trucks and freight cargo.

Cargo tank: A type of bulk packaging, a cargo tank has three distinct features:

• It is a tank designed to hold liquids, gases, and reinforcements.

• It is an attachment to the vehicle that can be permanent or temporary and can be loaded and unloaded without being detached from the main vehicle.

• It is not specifically designed for any tanker or cylinders.

Carrier: This refers to any individual or entity that transports goods or people by rail, air, car, or vessel.

Consignee: This is the person or company to whom the package is delivered.

EPA: An acronym for The Environmental Protection Agency.

FMCSR: An acronym for the Federal Motor Carrier Safety Regulations.

Freight container: This is any reusable container with a capacity of at least 64 cubic feet, specifically designed to be lifted with its contents intact. It is typically used to transport packages.

Fuel tank: This term refers to a container used to transport flammable or explosive liquid, as well as compressed gas, with the intention of delivering fuel to power the vehicle it's attached to, or other equipment on the transport vehicle.

Gross weight or mass: This refers to the weight of the package and its contents.

Hazard class: This term is used to classify a hazardous substance based on the criteria outlined in Sec. 172.01 Table regulations. A substance may meet the criteria for more than one hazard class, but it is only assigned to one.

Hazardous materials: This term refers to any solid, liquid, or gas that the government has identified as a potential risk to public safety or health. This includes water pollutants, toxic waste, and unstable substances.

Intermediate bulk container (IBC): This refers to any portable packaging that is rigid or flexible, designed to replace a portable tank or cylinder.

Non-bulk packaging: This is smaller than bulk packaging, with a capacity limit of 450 liters, or 119 gallons for liquids, and 400 kilograms or 882 pounds for solids.

NOS: An abbreviation for "not otherwise specified."

Portable tank: This term refers to bulk packaging with a maximum of 1,000 pounds that is not a tank car or cargo tank.

RQ: An abbreviation for reportable quantity.

Shipper's certification: This is a document that certifies the shipper has prepared and packaged the material in accordance with all relevant laws.

Chapter 5: Tank Vehicle (N) Endorsement

The tank endorsement license allows a driver to transport liquids in a designated cargo. This includes a wide range of liquids such as jet fuel, vehicle fuel, oil field liquids, fracking water, and milk. Essentially, this endorsement enables you to transport any form of liquid or gas. As you might anticipate, many of these substances necessitate a Hazardous Materials endorsement as well. This endorsement is marked with an 'N' on the Commercial Driver's License (CDL) to indicate the driver's qualification to operate these vehicles.

Every driver who transports a liquid or liquid gas in a tank with a capacity exceeding 119 gallons and a total capacity of 1,000 gallons or more is required to have this endorsement. However, an empty storage container tank of 1,000 gallons or more transported on a flatbed trailer is not classified as a tank vehicle, and the driver does not need a tank endorsement.

If you only possess a Commercial Learner's Permit (CLP), you are only permitted to operate a tank vehicle when it is empty. If the tanker has previously contained or transported hazardous material, it must be thoroughly cleaned before it can be transported again.

Before loading, unloading, or driving a tanker, it is crucial to inspect the vehicle for any safety concerns. As tankers vary in size and type, there may be specific components that require a detailed inspection. These components can be found in the vehicle's operator manual. It is recommended to read the manual to familiarize yourself with the characteristics of each tank.

The greatest concern with tankers is the potential for leaks. Therefore, it is of paramount importance to check for leaks. It is unsafe to load or unload a vehicle if there is a leak. Before loading, unloading, and at the beginning of any trip, you should always inspect the following parts of the vehicle for leaks:

1. The body or outer part for dents, cracks, or leaks.

2. The intake, discharge, and shut-off valves to ensure they are in the correct positions. Adjust the valves to the correct locations before loading, unloading, and driving.

3. All connections, pipes, and hoses for any signs of leakage, with particular attention to the joints.

4. Vents and manhole covers. Ensure gaskets are secure and closed correctly. Check that the vents are not blocked and are functioning correctly.

The vehicle you drive may be equipped with special-purpose equipment. As the driver, it is your responsibility to inspect and ensure it is functioning correctly. This may include vapor recovery kits, grounding and bonding cables, emergency shut-off systems, and built-in fire extinguishers. Never drive a vehicle with open valves or improperly closed manhole covers.

Before starting a trip, ensure the vehicle is equipped with the necessary emergency equipment. Double-check that you have all the required equipment and that it is functioning correctly.

Driving a tanker requires specific skills due to its higher center of gravity and the turbulence of the liquid. A tanker's center of gravity is higher than other commercial vehicles, making it top-heavy and more susceptible to rollovers, especially around curves. Research has shown that even at the legal speed limit for a curve, a tanker can still roll over. Therefore, exercise extreme caution on all highway curves, as well as exit and entrance ramps, and drive below the designated speed limit. Among all tankers, liquid tankers are the most likely to tip over and the easiest to overturn.

Understanding the Risks of Liquid Surge or Overflow

Liquid surge refers to the movement of liquid within a partially filled tank, which can potentially affect the vehicle's handling. This phenomenon is often observed when the vehicle comes to a halt, causing the liquid to oscillate back and forth, creating a wave-like motion inside the tank. When this wave reaches the tank's end, the liquid can exert significant force, potentially pushing the vehicle in the wave's direction.

This can pose a serious risk if the vehicle is on a slippery surface, such as ice. The force of the wave could propel the vehicle forward, potentially causing it to move further into an intersection or veer off the road.

Understanding Bulkheads

A bulkhead is a partition used to divide a liquid tank into smaller compartments. When loading cargo, it's crucial to distribute the weight evenly. Avoid overloading either the front or the rear of the vehicle.

What are Baffled Tanks?

A baffled tank is a tank fitted with bulkheads that have openings to allow liquid to flow from one compartment to another. This design helps control the forward and backward motion of a liquid surge. However, it doesn't prevent side-to-side surges.

Understanding Unbaffled Tanks

Also known as a smoothbore tank, this type of vehicle lacks any internal structures to regulate the flow of liquid. When operating one of these vehicles, be prepared for the potential of a strong surge.

Unbaffled tanks are typically used for transporting food products, such as milk. Due to the challenges of cleaning baffles, they are often avoided for sanitation purposes.

When operating an unbaffled tank, extreme caution is necessary, particularly when starting or stopping the vehicle.

Understanding Outage

Outage refers to the expansion of liquids as a result of increased temperature. Therefore, it's essential never to fill a cargo tank to its maximum capacity, leaving room for the liquid to expand.

Not all liquids expand at the same rate. Some expand more than others and require different outage allowances. As a driver, it's important to be aware of these differences.

Determining the Quantity to Load

If the liquid is extremely dense, like certain acids, a full tank may exceed the legal weight limit. Consequently, you may often need to fill tanks only to partial capacity. The permissible amount of liquid in the tank depends on several factors:

- The rate of expansion that will occur during transit
- The weight of the liquid
- Legal weight limits
- The temperature of the load

Tanker Driving Guidelines

A driver transporting more than 500 gallons of flammable liquid who exceeds the speed limit can be subjected to a minimum fine of $500, in addition to any other relevant penalties. If the driver has been previously convicted of this offense within the last two years, the fine escalates to $2,000, along with a potential suspension of their cargo tank and/or hazardous materials endorsement for up to six months.

Operating Hours

The maximum driving duration for a tanker carrying over 500 gallons is 20 hours within a work period when transporting flammable liquid.

While it's crucial to adhere to all road rules when operating any commercial vehicle, it's particularly important when driving a tanker. Here are some key rules to follow in different driving scenarios:

Braking

- Maintain a steady pressure on the brakes and avoid releasing them prematurely when stopping.
- Increase your following distance and start braking well in advance when stopping.
- If sudden braking is unavoidable, use controlled stab braking.
- Be careful when steering rapidly while braking, as there's a risk of rollover.
- Keep in mind the required stopping distance for your vehicle. This distance doubles on wet roads.
- Empty tankers may require a longer stopping distance than full ones.

Skidding

Oversteering, accelerating rapidly, or braking abruptly can lead to skidding. If your vehicle starts to skid, it may jackknife. Immediate action is necessary to regain wheel traction.

Curves

Given the tanker's higher center of gravity, you should slow down before entering a curve, then slightly accelerate while navigating through it. Remember, the posted speed limit for the curve might be too fast for a tanker.

Managing Liquid Surges

The most effective way to manage a liquid surge is to brake with consistent pressure. Stop gradually and maintain a generous distance between your vehicle and the one in front of you.

Personal Safety Gear Requirements

Operating a tank vehicle may necessitate supplementary fire and safety equipment based on the cargo being transported. This could include personal safety gear for the driver and specialized equipment for the tanks. It is incumbent upon the driver to understand what additional safety gear is needed and to ensure it is all in good working condition.

Potential Risks

Avoid transporting tanks that are leaking or spilling materials. Besides posing potential risks to the public, you could face penalties and be held accountable for cleaning up any spills. If you own the business, such incidents could even lead to its closure.

Connecting and Disconnecting Process

The four steps to connect a tanker are:

1. Inspect the trailer skid plate before connecting the main vehicle to the trailer.

You should be familiar with the dimensions of components like the fifth wheel, turntable, skid plate, jaw, and kingpin to identify any potential damage. Ensure the wedge and jaw are not lodged in the wheel's throat.

2. Position the parts by reversing the main vehicle directly in front of the trailer.

Using the vehicle's mirrors, align the sides and reverse until the rear mudguards align with the front of the trailer. Apply the parking brake, then exit the cabin and verify that the kingpin and fifth wheel are correctly aligned.

3. Test the trailer using a tug test.

To confirm the trailer is locked, engage the first gear and adjust the clutch to the friction point. The main vehicle should remain stationary. Apply the parking brake. Ensure the pull handle or coupling release lever is fully retracted, allowing the secondary locking latch to drop to a lower position.

After this, connect the air hoses and electrical cables. Verify the connection tabs are locked onto the joiners. Ensure all lights are working before you remove wheel chocks, if necessary.

4. Assess your work by returning the airbag level to its original position.

Conduct a second tug test by applying the trailer brakes and using the friction point in the first gear to confirm the trailer is securely hitched and the brakes are operational. Once done, proceed at a low speed in a straight line.

Perform a third tug test by applying pressure to the trailer brakes.

The four steps to disconnect a tank vehicle are:

1. Park the vehicle on the most level, firm surface available.

This is crucial to support the vehicle and its load. Apply the parking or maxi brakes on the main vehicle. Either chock the trailer's wheels or use spring brakes. If you need to reload the tank vehicle, apply chocks when parking on a slope. Check the front axle of the semi-trailer to ensure that if the landing legs bend, the rear axles will hold.

2. Detach the lines and cables from the vehicle.

Store them on the main vehicle. Avoid allowing dust or water to touch the tail shaft. Close all supply tabs. Lower the landing gear until the supports touch the ground. Visually confirm that both legs are lowered.

3. Raise the secondary safety latch to release the fifth wheel's jaw.

Move the handle forward to unlock it. Pull the handle as far as it will go. Engage the corner of the plate after pulling the handle and swinging it forward. If the release handle cannot be moved, the jaw is under load.

4. Move the vehicle approximately 20 centimeters (or eight inches) to release the main vehicle's parking brake.

Deflate the airbags to create a gap between the trailer skid plate and the top of the fifth wheel. The trailer should now rest on the landing gear. You can rectify the situation without causing damage to the system.

Tips for Tanker Endorsement

Operating tanker vehicles that transport gases and liquids necessitates specific endorsements based on the volume of the products being hauled. These endorsements become mandatory under the following conditions:

• If the total capacity of all the tanks on the vehicle is 1,000 gallons or more.

• If a single tank on the vehicle has a capacity exceeding 119 gallons.

• If the tank is used for transporting hazardous materials.

• If the tank is permanently or temporarily affixed to the vehicle.

• If the tank or all the tanks surpass either of the above-mentioned limits.

Flat bedding Exemption

A commercial vehicle that is transporting an empty storage container tank, not specifically designed for transport, is not classified as a tank vehicle when it is temporarily attached to a flatbed trailer.

Chapter 6: School Bus (S) Endorsement

Before attempting the school bus endorsement test, it's crucial to thoroughly acquaint yourself with both the state laws and the local school district regulations.

An individual possessing a Commercial Learner's Permit (CLP) with a passenger (P) endorsement and/or a school bus (S) endorsement is prohibited from operating a commercial vehicle unless a Commercial Driver's License (CDL) holder is present. The only passengers they are allowed to transport are fellow trainees, federal or state auditors, inspectors, and test examiners.

Understanding Mirror Usage and Danger Zones

A danger zone refers to any area around the school bus where students are at the highest risk of being struck by another vehicle or the school bus itself. Although the area 10 feet from the front bumper is considered the most hazardous for a student, the danger zone can extend up to 30 feet from the front bumper, 10 feet from either side of the bus, and 10 feet beyond the rear bumper.

The area to the left of the school bus should always be treated as one of the most perilous due to the potential risk of overtaking vehicles.

Adjusting the Mirrors on a School Bus

Properly positioning the mirrors on a school bus is crucial for the safe operation of the vehicle and for clear visibility of potential danger zones. Before driving any school bus, it is essential to check each mirror to ensure it offers the maximum possible viewing area. If necessary, make adjustments.

Flat Mirrors on the Left and Right Sides

Flat mirrors are located on the left and right corners of the bus, either at the side or the front of the windshield. These mirrors are used by the driver to monitor traffic, assess the clearance space, and check for students who may be near the sides or the back of the bus.

However, these mirrors do have blind spots immediately below and in front of them, as well as near the rear bumper. The size of the blind spot can vary depending on the length and width of the vehicle, ranging from as small as 50 feet to as large as 400 feet.

When adjusting these mirrors, ensure you can see:

- At least four bus lengths (approximately 200 feet) behind the bus

- Along both the right and left sides of the bus

- The rear tires of the bus, which should be fully on the ground

Convex Mirrors

Located immediately below the flat mirrors, the convex mirrors provide a wide-angle view of either side of the bus. These mirrors allow you to monitor traffic, the vehicle's clearance, and students along the sides of the bus. However, keep in mind that the reflections in the convex mirrors do not accurately represent the true size of objects and students.

When positioning the convex mirrors, ensure you can see:

- The entire side of the bus up to the mirror mounts

- The front of the rear tires, fully on the ground

- At least one traffic lane on both the left and right sides of the bus

Crossover Mirrors

Crossover mirrors are mounted on both the right and left front corners of the bus. These mirrors allow you to see the danger zone directly in front of the bus, which is not visible from the driver's seat. They also help you monitor the left- and right-side danger zones, including the service door and front wheel well area.

However, crossover mirrors can distort the size and distance of objects and individuals in relation to the bus.

For properly adjusted crossover mirrors, you should be able to see:

- The entire area in front of the bus, from the ground below the front bumper up to your normal field of view, with an overlap between your direct view and your mirror view
- The left and right tires fully on the ground
- The area in front of the bus extending back to the service door

All mirrors on the bus should be used systematically to ensure no student or object is in any danger zone.

Rearview Mirror

The overhead inside rearview mirror is mounted directly above the windshield on the driver's side. This mirror allows you to monitor passenger activity inside the bus and may provide limited visibility directly at the back of the vehicle if it has a glass-bottomed rear emergency door.

This mirror has two blind spots. The first is the area directly behind the driver's seat, and the second is a larger one that starts at the rear bumper and may extend up to 400 feet, depending on the bus model. Therefore, you should monitor traffic approaching and entering this area using the exterior side mirrors.

The overhead inside rearview mirror should be positioned so you can see:

- The top of the rear window in the bottom of the mirror

- All of the students, including the heads of those directly behind you.

Boarding and Alighting

Data indicates that students are more frequently fatally injured while boarding or alighting a school bus each year, compared to being a passenger. Therefore, it's crucial that you are familiar with the regulations concerning boarding and alighting students.

This segment provides a comprehensive overview, but it's not an exhaustive list of rules. Besides the information provided here, you should also familiarize yourself with all the state and local laws concerning approaching a school bus stop. These include the correct use of mirrors, alternating flashing lights, movable stop sign signals, and crossing control arms, if your bus is equipped with them.

When nearing a stop, adhere to these general guidelines:

- Approach the stop with caution, maintaining a slow speed.
- Always be vigilant for pedestrians, traffic, or any other obstacles before, during, and after you halt.
- Regularly check the mirrors.
- Activate the alternating flashing amber warning lights at least 200 feet or five to ten seconds before the stop, or as per the state law.

- Switch on the right turn signal indicator approximately 100 to 300 feet or three to five seconds before pulling over.
- Consistently check all mirrors, keeping an eye on the danger zones for students, traffic, and other objects.
- Move as far to the right on the traveled area of the road as possible.

Upon stopping, comply with the following rules:

- Bring the school bus to a complete halt with the front bumper at least 10 feet away from students. This allows you to monitor their movements more effectively.
- If the vehicle lacks a Park shift position, place the transmission in neutral and ensure the parking brake is engaged at every stop.
- Activate the alternating red lights when traffic is at a safe distance from the school bus and extend the stop arm.
- Confirm that all traffic has stopped before fully opening the door and signaling students to proceed.

Boarding Procedures

- The bus must be completely stationary before any student may board.
- Students should wait for the school bus at a designated location, facing the bus as it approaches.
- Students should only board after the driver signals that it's safe to do so.
- Regularly monitor the mirrors during boarding.
- Count the number of students at the stop to ensure everyone has boarded. If possible, learn the names of the students at

each stop. If a student is absent, inquire with the other students.

- Ensure students board in a single file line and at a slow pace, using the handrail.
- The dome light should be on when students are boarding in low light conditions.
- Do not move the bus until all students are seated and facing forward.
- Check all mirrors to ensure no one is rushing to catch the bus.
- If a student is missing, secure the bus, remove the key, and inspect around and beneath the vehicle.

Only when all students are accounted for should you depart. Follow this procedure:

- Close the door.
- Engage the transmission.
- Disengage the parking brake.
- Deactivate the alternating flashing red lights.
- Check the mirrors once more.
- Allow heavy traffic to disperse.
- Only when it is safe, move the bus, rejoin the traffic flow, and continue on the route.

Procedure for Boarding Students at the Campus

The process of boarding students at the campus is similar to their respective stops, with a few minor differences. These include:

- Switching off the vehicle's ignition

- Removing the key from the driver's area

- Positioning yourself in a way that you can oversee the boarding process

Procedure for Disembarking Students on the Route

When it's time to let the students off at their respective bus stops, adhere to the following routine:

- Stop completely at the designated bus stops

- Ensure that the students remain seated until you inform them it's safe to leave

- Keep an eye on all the mirrors

- Count the students getting off to verify their location before moving away from the stop

- Instruct the students to leave the bus and maintain a distance of at least 10 feet from the bus where you can see them clearly

- Check all mirrors again to ensure no students are nearby or returning to the bus

If a student is unaccounted for, take the following steps:

- Secure the bus

- Take the key

- Inspect around and beneath the vehicle

Once all students are accounted for, you can prepare to leave by following these steps:

- Shut the door

- Engage the transmission

- Release the parking brake

- Switch off the alternating flashing red lights

- Check all the mirrors

- Wait for the traffic to clear

- Only when it's safe, move the bus, rejoin the traffic, and continue the route

If a student's disembarking stop is missed, adhere to the local procedures of the school district.

Procedure for Students Who Must Cross the Street

When the bus is stopped either on a private road or a highway for boarding or disembarking students and the traffic isn't controlled by a traffic officer or a traffic control signal, follow these rules:

- Escort all students from prekindergarten through grade 8 who need to cross the road using the right-hand-held STOP sign

- Ensure all students cross in front of the bus

- Verify all students have crossed safely and that all other students and pedestrians are at a safe distance from the bus before starting the ignition

- As the school bus driver, you are obliged to enforce any state or local laws or recommendations related to the students' behavior outside of the bus

Procedure for Disembarking Students at School

These procedures serve as general guidelines. Each state and local entity has their own set of rules regarding the disembarking of students at school, school parking lot, or locations other than the roadway.

Make a safe, complete stop at the designated disembarking area and secure the bus through the following actions:

- Switch off the ignition

- Remove the key if you leave the driver's area

- Ensure the students remain seated until they're instructed to leave

- Position yourself to supervise the disembarking process

- Accompany all students from prekindergarten through grade 8 who must cross the highway or private road with an approved hand-held STOP sign

- Watch the students as they leave the bus to ensure they promptly move away from the disembarking area

- Double-check the bus for students who may be hiding or sleeping and for any items left behind

- Check all mirrors to ensure no students are returning to the bus

- If the bus is secure and a student is unaccounted for outside of the vehicle, take the key and inspect around and beneath the bus

Once all the students have been accounted for, you can prepare to leave by following these steps:

- Close the door

- Fasten the seat belt

- Start the engine

- Engage the transmission

- Release the parking brake

- Switch off the alternating flashing red lights

- Turn on the left turn signal

- Check all the mirrors, again

- Wait for the traffic to clear

- Only when it is safe, pull away from the disembarking area.

Risks During School Bus Loading and Unloading

Maintain a vigilant watch on the students as they approach the school bus. It's crucial to keep track of each student, especially if one suddenly disappears from view. It's not rare for a student to drop an item near the bus during the loading or unloading process. If a student stoops to pick up the dropped item, they might be in a blind spot at a risky moment. Advise students to leave the fallen item and move to a safe distance from the bus, away from danger zones. They should then signal you to retrieve the item for them.

Potential Hazards with Handrails

There's a risk of clothing, accessories, or even parts of a student's body getting entangled in the handrail or the door while exiting the bus. Such incidents have, in some cases, led to injuries and even fatalities. Therefore, it's essential to closely monitor the students as they disembark the bus and ensure they are in a safe location before you drive away.

Post-trip Inspection

After completing your route or any school-related activity, a post-trip inspection is mandatory. Conduct a thorough walkthrough of the bus to check for:

- Forgotten items
- Students who might have fallen asleep
- Open windows and doors
- Mechanical issues, such as flashing warning lights, mirror systems, or malfunctioning stop signals
- Any signs of damage or vandalism

Emergency Preparedness

The initial step in any emergency response is to ascertain whether an evacuation of the bus is necessary. The ideal response is to keep the students on the bus, ensuring their safety and preventing a challenging situation from escalating. Before initiating any evacuation, it is crucial to determine the most suitable course of action.

It is essential to differentiate between the threat of a fire and an actual fire, as well as between a fuel spill and the mere smell of fuel. Carefully assess the situation before deciding to evacuate the students, as this could potentially expose them to greater danger.

However, there are four circumstances where evacuation is mandatory:

1. When there is a real or apparent threat of fire.

2. If the bus abruptly halts near or on a railway crossing.

3. If an imminent collision necessitates evacuation.

4. In the event of a hazardous material spill.

Evacuation Guidelines

While no one wishes to be in such a situation, prior planning can facilitate a smooth evacuation. If feasible, assign at least two older students to each emergency exit to assist others in exiting the bus. Designate another older student to guide the students to a safe location post-evacuation.

In the absence of older students, it is your responsibility to explain the emergency evacuation procedures to all the students and ensure their understanding. They should be aware of the emergency exits and how to operate them. Moreover, they need to comprehend the importance of adhering to your instructions.

Here are some tips on identifying a safe location in case of a school bus evacuation:

- Keep all students at least 100 feet away from the road, particularly from oncoming traffic, to minimize the risk of accidents or injury from debris if another vehicle hits the bus.

- If the bus is on fire, guide the students upwind and away from smoke and flames.

- If the bus is near or on railway tracks, lead the students as far away from the tracks and approaching trains as possible.

- In case of a hazardous materials spill, guide the students upwind and at least 300 feet away from the bus.

- If the bus is in the direct path of a tornado and evacuation is ordered, lead the students to a nearby ditch or culvert if no building is available. Instruct them to lie face down with their hands covering their heads. Ensure you're far enough from the bus to avoid it toppling over the students. Avoid areas prone to flash floods.

Evacuation Procedures

Here is a summary of the steps to follow if you need to evacuate the students from the school bus:

1. Identify the type of evacuation required, such as front or rear door, a combination of doors, or window or roof.

2. Secure the bus by placing the transmission in Park or neutral, engaging the parking brakes, turning off the engine and removing the key, and activating the hazard warning lights.

3. If time permits, inform the dispatch office about the location, conditions prompting the evacuation, and the assistance required.

4. If possible, place the radio microphone or phone out of the driver's window for later use if operable.

5. If the radio is unavailable or inoperable, request help from a passing motorist or a nearby resident. As a last resort, send two responsible older students to seek help. Always stay with the students.

6. Evacuate the students from the bus, avoiding moving anyone with potential neck or spinal injuries unless their life is in immediate danger.

7. Assign an older student to lead others away from the bus to the nearest safe location.

8. Check the entire bus to ensure all students have evacuated.

9. Retrieve the emergency first aid box, equipment, and supplies.

10. Join the students, ensuring everyone is accounted for and assessing their health and safety.

11. Set out emergency warning devices at the scene in appropriate positions.

12. Prepare information for emergency personnel, including a description of the incident, the condition of the students, and any other relevant information.

Safety Guidelines for School Bus Drivers

Utilizing Strobe Lights

Many school buses are fitted with white strobe lights on the roof. Their purpose is to enhance visibility during nighttime.

Navigating in Stormy Weather

Controlling the steering wheel becomes challenging when strong winds hit the bus, potentially pushing it off the road. Here are four tips for managing the bus in such situations:

1. Firmly hold the steering wheel. Regardless of the wind's intensity, maintain a strong grip.

2. Predict the wind's direction. Make necessary turns to avoid a direct hit from the wind.

3. Lower the vehicle's speed. This action will decrease the wind's effect. If necessary, pull over and wait for the wind to calm down. Prioritizing students' safety over punctuality is always the right choice.

4. If you're uncertain about what to do next, contact the dispatcher for advice.

Reversing a School Bus

Reversing a school bus should be your last option. Only do it when there's no safer and better way to maneuver the vehicle. Never reverse the bus when students are outside. If reversing is unavoidable, adhere to the following steps:

- Request someone to serve as a lookout. Their job is to alert you if you're at risk of colliding with something. However, they're not responsible for instructing you on how to steer the vehicle.
- Ask the students to stay silent during this time to ensure you can hear the lookout.
- Utilize all the vehicle's mirrors.
- Reverse slowly. Avoid rushing as an unexpected object or person might appear.
- If no lookout is available, park the bus, switch off the engine, and remove the keys. Exit the vehicle and inspect the area behind the bus to ensure the path is clear.

Chapter 7: Air Brakes

Air brakes, commonly used in large commercial vehicles, are a reliable and safe stopping mechanism. Unlike hydraulic brakes, they utilize a combination of air and spring pressure. The air is drawn from the environment and compressed in the vehicle's air compressor until the storage tank reaches a pressure of 120 psi.

The convenience of air brakes lies in their easy installation and removal, and the absence of fluids that can potentially run out, as in the case of hydraulic brakes. Moreover, they offer controlled pressure and have backup air tanks to ensure functionality even if the compressor fails or there is an air leak.

Air brakes are generally categorized into two primary systems: the supply system and the control system.

The Supply System

As the name suggests, the supply system delivers air to the brakes. It consists of several components, including:

Air Compressor

The air compressor functions as the air pump for the storage tank. It is typically connected to the engine through a V-belt or occasionally, a gear set. The compressor may have its own oil supply or rely on the engine oil for lubrication. If it has its own supply, it's crucial to ensure that the oil levels are sufficient before embarking on a journey.

The compressor pressurizes the storage containers by forcing air into them. This air is then pushed through an opening in the tank, resulting in the buildup of pressure. When the compressed air is released, it can be harnessed as energy. The compressor is powered by an engine that transforms electrical energy into kinetic energy, similar to a combustion engine, and includes components like a crankshaft, valve, piston, head, and a connecting rod.

Positive and Dynamic Displacement

Air compression is achieved through two methods: positive and dynamic displacement. Both have numerous subcategories and, while they achieve the same result, they do so through different processes.

Positive Displacement

This method compresses air in a small-capacity chamber. These compressors are versatile and can be used in a wide range of environments, from industrial applications to personal use.

Dynamic Displacement Compressors

Dynamic displacement compressors generate airflow through a rotating blade powered by an engine. The air is forced into a confined space to create pressure, and the compressor retains this kinetic energy. These compressors are particularly useful in chemical or steel plants. There are two types of dynamic displacement: axial and centrifugal.

Air Compressor Governor

The air compressor governor is responsible for controlling the amount of air pumped into the storage tank. When the tank is full, the governor intervenes to stop the compressor from pumping more air. Conversely, when the air level is low, the governor allows more air into the tank.

The storage tank, also known as the reservoir, is where the compressed air is stored. The size of the tank can vary depending on the vehicle. If the compressor fails, the air in the tank can still operate the brakes temporarily.

Typically, air storage tanks have a pressure rating of 150 to 200 psi.

Air Tank Drain

As the name suggests, an air tank drain allows the accumulated fluid in the compressed air to be drained. Any amount of accumulation can cause brake failure if it freezes in cold conditions.

An air tank can drain automatically or manually. In automatic draining, an integrated electric heating device prevents the water from freezing. For manual draining, you simply pull the air tank cable.

Alcohol Evaporator

Some air brake systems feature an alcohol evaporator that introduces alcohol into the air system. This alcohol helps to prevent ice formation. During cold weather, it's advisable to regularly check and refill the alcohol container if necessary.

However, the presence of alcohol in the system does not negate the need for regular air tank draining.

Safety Valve

The air compressor fills an initial tank equipped with a safety valve. This valve serves as a protective measure against dangerously high pressure in the system. The valve opens when the air pressure reaches 150 psi, indicating a potential issue within the system.

A smaller reservoir, known as a purge, is included in the air brake's supply system. This reservoir holds and purifies the air. The supply reservoir then stores the air and distributes it to the parking brake reservoir, primary and secondary reservoirs, as well as the auxiliary air supply distribution point.

The Control Mechanism

The control mechanism consists of a variety of elements, which are detailed below.

Brake Pedal

The brake is activated by pressing the brake pedal. The force exerted on the pedal determines the pressure level. When the brake pedal is released, air escapes from the tank, reducing the pressure. The air compressor then has to replenish the lost air. If the brake is frequently pressed and released without necessity, the air compressor may not have sufficient time to refill, potentially resulting in brake failure.

Foundation Brakes

Foundation brakes are installed on every wheel and typically come in four types.

1. Brake Drums, Linings, Shoes

Each wheel is connected at the rear to the brake drum. The braking mechanism inside the drum is activated when the brake shoes and linings are pressed against the drum, generating friction and heat. Overuse of the shoes and lining can cause damage.

2. S-cam Brakes

In the S-cam brake system, named for its shape, air enters each brake chamber when the pedal is pressed. The air pressure pulls the rod off, causing the slack adjuster to move and the camshaft to rotate, spinning the s-cam. The s-cam then separates the brake pads and presses them onto the drum brake. The process is reversed when the brake pedal is released.

3. Wedge Brakes

In this system, the brake chamber's pushrod drives a wedge between the ends of the two brake pads, causing them to separate and press into the drum. This system may have one or two brake chambers and may adjust automatically or manually.

4. Disc Brakes

Disc brakes function similarly to the s-cam brakes, but instead of the s-cam, there is a power screw. When the screw rotates, it tightens the disc or rotor that is sandwiched between the brake lining pads of a caliper.

Supply-Pressure Gauge

Connected to the air tank in all vehicles with air brakes, the supply-pressure gauge shows the pressure level in the air tanks. Each section of the dual air brake system has a gauge.

Application Pressure Gauges

This type of air brake is typically found on buses. The pressure gauge is connected to the air valve and displays the pressure in the tank. If a vehicle has a dual air brake, it could have a gauge for each system or one gauge with two needles. The gauge shows the air pressure applied to the brakes. If you need to increase the application pressure to maintain the same speed, the brakes are fading. You should slow down the vehicle and shift to a lower gear. The need for increased pressure could also indicate that the brakes are out of adjustment, there are air leaks, or there may be mechanical problems.

Low Air Pressure Warning

Vehicles with air brakes provide warning signals before the pressure drops below 60 psi. The warning can be a red light, an alarm, or a wigwag, depending on the vehicle. The wigwag lowers a mechanical arm to eye level when the pressure drops to 60 psi and raises when the pressure exceeds that. Larger buses typically provide this signal between 80 to 85 psi.

Stop Light Switch

The stop light switch alerts the driver behind you that you're applying the brakes. In the air brake system, this is accomplished with an electric switch that is sensitive to air pressure. When you apply the brakes, the switch activates the brake lights.

Front Brake Limiting Valve

Vehicles manufactured before 1975 have a front brake limiting valve with a control in the cab. These limiting valves were used to reduce the likelihood of front wheel skids on slippery surfaces by reducing the vehicle's stopping power. The control is marked with "normal" and "slippery." When the control is set to "slippery," the limiting valve cuts the "normal" air pressure to the front brakes by half. Later tests revealed that front-wheel skids from braking are unlikely, even on ice. If you drive one of these vehicles, ensure the control is set to "normal" for full stopping power. Many vehicles have automatic front-wheel limiting valves, which reduce the air to the front brakes unless they're applied very hard, such as with 60 psi or more. This valve is not under the driver's control.

Spring Brakes and Emergency Brakes

Every bus, tractor, and truck should be equipped with both emergency and parking brakes. It's essential that these brakes are mechanically driven as air pressure can dissipate over time. Spring brakes serve this purpose.

When the vehicle is in motion, the robust springs are restrained by air pressure. Once this pressure is removed, the springs activate the brakes. The driver can control the parking brake from the cab, allowing them to release the air from the spring brakes, thus activating them. If there's a leak in the system causing a loss of air, the spring brakes will automatically activate.

When the air pressure in tractors and straight trucks drops to between 20 to 45 psi, the spring brakes fully engage. However, it's advisable not to wait for the brakes to activate automatically. As soon as the low air-pressure warning light and buzzer activate, the vehicle should be brought to a safe stop while the brakes are still under control.

The effectiveness of spring brakes depends on their adjustment. If they're not properly adjusted, neither the regular brakes nor the emergency and parking brakes will function correctly.

In modern vehicles equipped with air brakes, the parking brake is controlled by a yellow, diamond-shaped push-pull knob. To apply the parking brakes, pull the knob out, and to release them, push it in. In older vehicles, a lever may control the parking brakes. These should be used whenever the vehicle is parked.

It's crucial not to depress the brake pedal while the spring brakes are activated. The combined force of the spring and air pressure could damage the system. While many brake systems are designed to prevent this, not all are.

Modulating Control Valves

Some vehicles come with a modulating valve; a control handle located on the dashboard. This is used to gradually apply the spring brakes. It's spring-loaded, providing a tactile sense of the braking action. The further the lever is moved, the harder the brakes are applied. This design allows you to control the spring brakes if the service brakes fail. When parking a vehicle with one of these valves, move the lever as far as possible and secure it with the locking device.

Dual Parking Control Valves

Spring brakes activate when the main air pressure is lost. Some vehicles, especially buses, come with a separate air tank that can be used to release the spring brakes, allowing the vehicle to be moved in an emergency.

One of the valves is a push-pull type, used to apply the spring brakes for parking. The other valve is spring-loaded in the "out" position. When the control is pushed in, air from the separate tank releases the spring brakes, enabling the vehicle to move.

When the button is released, the spring brakes reactivate. The separate air tank only has enough air for a few applications, so careful planning is needed when moving the vehicle. Otherwise, you may find yourself stopped in a hazardous location when the separate air supply is depleted.

Anti-Lock Braking Systems (ABS)

The Anti-lock Braking System (ABS) is designed to prevent the wheels of a vehicle from seizing up during intense braking. To ascertain if the vehicle you're operating is equipped with ABS, refer to the certification label for the manufacturing date.

If your vehicle is equipped with ABS, it's crucial to remember the following points:

• A yellow malfunction light serves as a warning if any component is not working correctly.

• The ABS malfunction lamp is situated on the instrument panel in all tractors, trucks, and buses.

• On trailers, the yellow malfunction lamp can be located either at the front or the back corners on the left side.

• Dollies produced after March 1, 1998, must have the yellow malfunction lamp installed on the left side.

• The malfunction light operates differently depending on the vehicle. For newer models, the light illuminates briefly at start-up then quickly extinguishes. On older models, the light remains on until the vehicle exceeds 5 mph.

• If the lamp remains on after the bulb check or illuminates while the vehicle is in motion, it may indicate a loss of ABS control on one or more wheels.

• Identifying if towed vehicles manufactured before DOT requirements have ABS can be challenging. Inspect the vehicle's electronic control unit (ECU) and wheel speed sensor wires originating from the rear of the brakes.

• ABS does not function like standard brakes. The system neither enhances nor diminishes normal braking capability. It is only activated when the wheels are at risk of locking up.

• ABS does not necessarily reduce the vehicle's stopping distance but aids in maintaining vehicle control during hard braking.

Dual Air Brake Systems

Most commercial vehicles come equipped with dual air brake systems. These systems consist of two separate air brake systems operated by a single set of brake controls. Each system has its own air, tanks, hoses, and lines. One system controls the regular brakes on the rear axles, while the other operates the brakes on the front axle (and occasionally one rear axle). Both systems supply air to the trailer and are known as primary and secondary systems.

Before embarking on a journey with a dual-system vehicle, allow time for the air compressor to build to 100 psi in both the primary and secondary systems. Monitor both pressure gauges closely. If the system indicators are needles, there will be two needles in one gauge.

Pay particular attention to the low-air pressure warning light and buzzer. These should deactivate when the air pressure in both systems exceeds 60 psi or the value set by the vehicle's manufacturer.

These indicators activate before the air pressure falls below 60 psi in either system. If one system has low pressure, it indicates that either the front or rear brakes are not functioning correctly, which will increase your stopping distance. If you encounter this issue, safely stop the vehicle and have the system repaired.

Effective Use of Air Brakes

For a standard stop, gently press the brake pedal to bring the vehicle to a safe, smooth halt. If your vehicle has a manual transmission, wait until the engine rpm is near idle before engaging the clutch. Once the vehicle has stopped, shift into a gear.

Braking forcefully on a slippery surface without ABS could potentially lock the steering wheels, causing loss of steering control. There's also a risk that the other wheels may lock up, leading to skidding, jackknifing, or even spinning of the vehicle.

ABS is designed to prevent such incidents. The system's computer detects when wheel lock is imminent and adjusts the braking pressure to a safe level, allowing you to maintain control.

Even if ABS is only installed on the tractor, the trailer, or a single axle, it still offers control. You should continue to brake as usual.

If only the tractor has ABS, you should still be able to maintain steering control. ABS also minimizes the likelihood of jackknifing. However, you should still monitor the trailer and ease off the brakes if it starts to swing out.

When only the trailer has ABS, it's less likely to swing out. But if you lose steering control or the vehicle starts to jackknife, ease off the brakes until you regain control.

When operating a tractor-trailer with ABS, remember the following:

• Apply only the necessary force to stop safely and maintain control.

• The braking method remains the same with ABS, whether it's on the tractor, trailer, or both.

• Monitor the tractor and trailer when slowing down, and ease off the brakes to maintain control.

• If all axles of a straight truck or combination have ABS, you can fully apply the brakes during an emergency stop.

• If the ABS fails, you still have conventional brakes.

Emergency Braking

If a vehicle suddenly cuts in front of you, the instinctive reaction is to brake. This is only effective if there's sufficient distance to stop and the brakes are used correctly.

Always brake in a manner that keeps the vehicle in a straight line and allows you to steer if necessary. You can choose between two methods: controlled or stab braking.

Controlled braking involves applying the brakes as hard as possible without locking the wheels. Keep steering wheel movements minimal. If the wheels lock, release the brakes and reapply them as soon as possible.

Stab braking involves fully applying the brakes and releasing them when the wheels lock up. As soon as the wheels start to roll, apply the brakes fully again. It may take up to a second for the wheels to start rolling after releasing the brakes.

If you reapply the brakes before the wheels start moving, the vehicle won't straighten out.

Understanding Stopping Distance

Stopping distance refers to the time it takes for a vehicle to come to a complete halt once the brake pedal is pressed. While hydraulically powered brakes respond immediately, air brakes experience a slight delay. This delay, typically around half a second, is due to the time it takes for the air to travel through the lines to the brakes.

The overall stopping distance for vehicles equipped with air brakes is influenced by four key factors:

• The distance covered during the driver's perception time

• The distance covered during the driver's reaction time

• The distance covered during the brake lag time

• The distance covered during effective braking

When a vehicle is moving at 55 mph on a dry pavement, the air brake lag distance adds approximately 32 feet. This means that, at this speed, an average driver with good traction and brakes requires a total stopping distance of over 450 feet. To put this into perspective, that's equivalent to one and a half football fields.

Understanding Brake Failure or Fading

Brakes are engineered to function by having brake shoes or pads rub against the drum or disc, a process that generates heat. While brakes are designed to withstand a significant amount of heat, they can still fail or fade if they become excessively heated, often due to overuse.

Brake fade is a phenomenon caused by excessive heating, which triggers chemical changes in the brake lining. These changes diminish the amount of friction, impeding the braking process. Brake fade can also lead to the expansion of the brake drums.

As the overheated drum expands, the shoes and linings have to travel a greater distance to make contact with the drums. This reduces the force of the contact. Persistent overuse of brakes can exacerbate brake fade to the point where the vehicle cannot be slowed down or stopped.

Brake fade can also be influenced by brake adjustment. For a safe stop, each brake must contribute equally to the braking effort. When brakes are out of adjustment, they may stop working effectively before the properly adjusted ones, causing the latter to overheat and eventually fade. This can leave you with insufficient braking power to control the vehicle. Brakes can fall out of adjustment quite rapidly, so regular checks are essential.

Chapter 8: Vehicle Inspection

As a driver, it's your responsibility to conduct daily vehicle inspections to identify potential problems or defects before they escalate into significant issues that could compromise safety.

Legally, you're required not only to carry out these daily inspections but also to maintain a written record of your vehicle's maintenance and ensure clear communication about its safety status.

The inspection report serves as a crucial tool for drivers to communicate information to the carrier and, most importantly, the carrier's maintenance department. The reports you complete are vital as they confirm that inspections have been conducted, record any defects, and confirm that necessary repairs have been made.

Both federal and state governments enforce laws requiring these inspections and have the authority to declare a vehicle "out of service" if deemed unsafe.

Vehicles that Require Inspections:

Which vehicles require daily inspections?

Provincially regulated carriers are required to conduct daily inspections on the following vehicles:

- Trucks registered with a minimum weight of 11,794 kilograms.

- Commercial passenger vehicles with a seating capacity of at least 11 passengers, including the driver.

Federally regulated carriers must complete trip inspection reports on:

- Trucks registered with a minimum weight of 4,500 kilograms.

- Commercial passenger vehicles with a seating capacity of at least 11, including the driver.

Types of Inspections:

It's important to be familiar with the three types of vehicle inspections:

Pre-trip Inspection:

This inspection involves a thorough check of the vehicle's engine and other parts before the start of every trip. The aim is to prevent potential breakdowns and accidents.

During-trip Inspection:

This is an informal inspection conducted during the trip. The driver should be vigilant about the vehicle's performance and be alert to any signs that something might be wrong. This could include unusual sights, smells, or sounds. The driver should also periodically stop to check critical parts of the vehicle, such as:

- Tires, wheels, rims
- Lights, reflectors
- Brakes
- Electrical connections
- Trailer coupling devices
- Cargo securement devices

Post-trip Inspection and Report:

At the end of the trip, it's crucial for the driver to inspect the vehicle again. They may need to file a report about the engine and other parts that require repair.

The 7-Step Inspection Guide

This comprehensive pre-trip inspection procedure ensures that all crucial aspects of the vehicle are thoroughly checked. The seven steps include:

1. Vehicle Overview

2. Engine Compartment

3. Cab Interior

4. Lights

5. External Walk-around Inspection

6. Signal Lights

7. Brake System

Each step is detailed as follows:

1. Vehicle Overview:

This initial step involves a general assessment of the vehicle's condition. Start by reviewing the previous driver's report and examining the overall state of the vehicle. Check for any leaks and assess the wear and tear underneath the vehicle. Ensure that no obstructions are present when it's time to depart. If you notice anything unusual, have it repaired before commencing your trip.

2. Engine Compartment:

During this step, ensure the parking brakes are engaged and the wheels are chocked. Check all fluid levels, including oil, coolant, battery fluids, automatic transmission fluid, and windshield wiper fluid. You might need to start the engine to check the transmission fluid. Make sure there are no leaks in the compartment, inspect the belts for wear and tightness, and examine the engine's electrical wiring for any signs of wear or cracks. Finally, secure the hood, cab, or engine compartment door.

3. Cab Interior:

This step involves checking all necessary aspects inside the vehicle, as outlined below:

a. Start the engine, ensuring the parking brake is engaged and the gearshift is in neutral (manual transmission) or park (automatic transmission). Listen for any unusual noises.

b. Check the ABS (anti-lock braking system) indicator lights. The dashboard light should come on and then turn off. If it doesn't, the ABS might be malfunctioning. For trailers, if the yellow light on the left rear doesn't turn off, the ABS might be malfunctioning.

c. Check gauges for oil pressure readings, air pressure, ammeter or voltmeter, coolant temperature, engine oil temperature, and warning lights and buzzers.

d. Check controls for any loose or incorrect settings or damage, including the clutch, steering wheel, gas pedal, brake controls, foot brake, parking brakes, trailer brakes (if applicable), retarder controls (if applicable), interaxle differential lock, horns, windshield wipers/washers, lights, headlights, dimmer switch, turn signals, 4-way flashers, and parking clearance identification marker switches.

e. Check the windshield and mirrors for any cracks, dirt, or debris that could obstruct your view. Clean and adjust them if necessary.

f. Check for safety/emergency equipment, including spare electrical fuses (unless the vehicle has a built-in circuit breaker), three red reflective triangles, six fuses, three liquid burning flares, and a properly charged and rated fire extinguisher.

4. Lights:

This step involves ensuring the parking brake is set. When you turn off the engine, remember to take the key with you.

5. Comprehensive Vehicle Inspection

Upon setting the parking brake and ensuring you have the keys, the fifth step in the inspection process commences. This involves verifying the following:

Ensure the low beam lights and flashers are functioning correctly.

Check that the high beam lights are operational.

Turn off the headlights and emergency flashers.

Activate the parking, clearance, side-marker, and identification lights, along with the right turn signal.

This inspection should be conducted on all sides and corners of the vehicle in the following sequence, if possible:

• General

- Left front side

- Left front suspension

- Left front brake

- Front

- Right side

- Condition of visible parts

- Cargo securements

- Right rear

- Rear

- Left side

Additional conditions that require inspection include:

- Lights, reflectors, glass, and windshield

- Vehicle doors and accessories

- Wheels, tires, and accessories

- Fuel tanks and fluid levels

- Shock absorbers, springs, nuts, and bolts

- Axle and steering mechanism

- Correct color of lightings

- Safe cab locks

- Check for leaks, wear, misalignments, and other damages

- Cargo

- Sideboards

- Canvas or tarps (if applicable)

- Electrical wirings, air lines, tire racks, exhaust systems

- Spare parts

The following checklist aids in ensuring all areas are prepared for the journey:

1. Overview

a. Conduct a thorough inspection of the vehicle.

b. Clean lights, reflectors, and glass.

2. Left front side

a. Clean the driver's door glass.

b. Ensure door latches and locks are functional.

c. Check for bent or broken studs.

d. Verify wheels have all their rims.

e. Ensure clamps lugs are correctly aligned.

f. Check tire inflation.

g. Verify tire caps and valve stems are operational.

h. Check for significant tire damage.

i. Verify there are no loose or rusted nuts.

j. Check the hub oil level is within normal limits and free of leaks.

3. Left front suspension

a. Inspect the spring, spring hangers, shackles, and U-bolts.

b. Verify the shock absorber is in good condition.

4. Left front brake

a. Ensure the brake drum is in good condition.

b. Verify the House is in good condition.

5. Front

a. Check the front axle's condition.

b. Ensure the steering mechanism has no loose, damaged, or missing parts.

c. Clean the windshield and check for damages.

d. Verify the windshield wiper arms have the proper spring tension.

e. Check the wiper blades are secure and undamaged.

f. Check the parking lights and identification lights. They should be amber and function properly.

g. Verify the right front turn signal is clean and operational.

6. Right side

a. Check the same items as the left side.

b. Ensure the cab locks are engaged for the cab over the engine.

c. Verify the right front fuel tank is securely mounted, undamaged, and not leaking.

d. Check the fuel crossover line is secure.

e. Ensure the fuel tank is adequately filled.

f. Verify the tank cap is securely on.

7. Visible parts

a. Ensure the transmission has no leaks.

b. Verify the rear of the engine is not leaking.

c. Ensure the air line and wirings are secure.

d. Ensure the exhaust system is secure with no leaks.

e. Verify the exhaust system is not touching the wiring or the air lines.

f. Check for damage to the spare tire carrier or rack.

g. Ensure the spare tire and wheel are securely mounted on the rack.

h. Verify the spare tire and wheel are the proper size and inflated correctly.

8. Cargo securement

a. Verify the cargo is properly secured, including the block and brace, and that it's tied or chained correctly.

b. Ensure the header board is adequate. Secure it if necessary.

c. Verify the side-boards and stakes are strong, undamaged, and properly placed.

d. Ensure the canvas or tarp is secured properly to prevent tearing or billowing and doesn't obstruct the mirrors.

e. If the vehicle is oversized, confirm all the appropriate flags, lamps, and reflectors are properly mounted and all required permits are in your possession.

f. Ensure the curbside cargo compartment doors are functional and securely closed or latched. Also, ensure the required security seals are in place.

9. Right rear

a. Verify the wheels and rims are present, with no broken or bent spaces, studs, clamps, or lugs.

b. Ensure the tires are properly inflated, and the valve stems and caps are in good condition.

c. Check the tires for serious damage.

d. Verify there is nothing stuck between the tires.

e. Ensure the tires aren't rubbing against each other.

f. Verify the wheel bearings are not leaking.

g. Ensure the suspension spring, hangers, shackles, and U-bolts are in good condition. Verify the axle is secure and the powered axle is not leaking.

h. Check the torque rod arms and bushings are in good condition.

i. Verify the shock absorbers are in good condition.

j. Check the air ride components are in good condition.

k. Check the brake adjustments, as well as the brake drums and brake disks.

l. Verify the hose has not excessive wear.

m. Ensure the side marker lights are clean and operational. Verify the lights are the proper color, with a red at rear and all others amber.

n. Ensure the side marker reflectors are also clean and the proper color, red in the rear, and all others amber.

6. Signal lights

The next step is to verify the signal lights are not only functional but also conform to requirements. This checklist will guide you through this part of the inspection.

1. In-vehicle inspection

a. Turn off all the lights.

b. Activate the stop lights, and apply the trailer hand brake, or have someone apply the brake pedal.

c. Activate the left turn signal.

2. Out-of-vehicle inspection

a. Ensure the left front turn signal is clean, operational, and displaying the correct color. It should be amber or white on the signals facing front.

b. Verify the left rear turn signal is clean, functional, and displaying the correct color. It should be red, amber, or yellow.

3. In-vehicle inspection

a. Turn off the lights not needed for driving.

b. Check all the required trip manifests, permits, and any other paperwork required for the trip is in the vehicle.

c. Secure any loose articles in the cab that may interfere with the controls or hit the driver in an accident.

d. Start the engine.

7. Brake System

Start this process by igniting the engine and ensuring there are no hydraulic leaks. Here's a step-by-step guide to assist you with the procedure.

1. Inspection of Hydraulic Brakes

a. If the vehicle is fitted with hydraulic brakes, depress the brake pedal thrice.

b. Maintain a strong pressure on the brake pedal for a duration of five seconds.

If the pedal exhibits any movement, it could suggest a leak or another issue with the brake system.

c. If the pedal does exhibit movement, refrain from operating the vehicle until the issue is rectified.

2. Checking the Parking Brake

a. Secure the safety belt.

b. Engage the parking brake for a power-only unit.

c. Disengage the trailer's parking brake if it's equipped with one.

d. Switch the vehicle into low gear.

e. Gently move forward against the parking brake to test its holding capacity.

f. Repeat this process with the trailer parking brake engaged and power unit until the parking brakes disengage, if applicable.

3. Testing the Service Brake

a. Operate the vehicle at an approximate speed of 5 mph.

b. Apply a strong pressure to the brake.

c. If the vehicle veers to one side, it could suggest a problem with the brakes.

d. If you experience anything unusual when you apply the brake or if the vehicle exhibits a delayed response in stopping, it suggests a problem with the brake system. Refrain from operating the vehicle until the issue is rectified.

Potential Tire Concerns

When examining the tires, it's crucial to be aware of several potential issues and key areas. Here are the main points to consider:

• Uneven tire wear. The front tires should have a tread depth of at least 4/32 of an inch in each groove, while the remaining tires should have a groove depth of at least 2/32 of an inch. No fabric material should be visible on the sidewall or tread.

- The tires should not be underinflated or overinflated.

- Tread separation.

- Any cuts or damages to the tires.

- Inconsistent tire sizes.

- Dual tires that are in close proximity to each other or any other part of the vehicle.

- Wheel and rim problems.

- Damaged rims.

- Ensure the wheel nuts are secure. Rust around the wheel nuts could suggest a loose nut. After a tire replacement, drive a short distance and then verify the nuts are tight.

- Misaligned, twisted, or cracked lock rings, which could be hazardous.

- Cracked drums.

- Faulty brake drums or shoes.

- Worn brake shoes that are dangerously thin or are missing or broken.

- Brake pads or shoes contaminated with brake fluid, grease, or oil.

- Steering system problems.

- The steering wheel should not deviate more than 10 degrees from the center. This can make steering difficult.

- Bent, broken, or defective tie rods, steering column, or steering gearbox.

- Misplaced cotter keys, bolts, and nuts.

- For power steering units, there should be no leaking or broken hoses or pumps. Check fluid levels.

Suspension System Concerns

The suspension system not only binds the vehicle and its load but also maintains the axles' alignment. Issues in this area, such as broken components, can be extremely dangerous. It's crucial to inspect this area for any problems, defects, or abnormalities. Look for the following issues:

• Cracked or broken spring hangers, which are essential for the correct positioning and movement of the axle.

• Damaged leaves in a multi-leaf spring or leaf shifting that comes into contact with a tire or any other part of the vehicle.

• Missing or damaged leaves in any leaf spring.

• If a quarter or more of the leaves are missing, the vehicle is considered "out of service." However, any smaller defect could still pose a risk.

• Leaking shock absorbers.

• Damaged or leaking air suspension systems.

• Cracked, damaged, or missing torque rod or arm, spring hangers, U-bolts, or other axle-positioning parts.

• Loose, broken, cracked, or missing frame members.

• Steering system issues.

Inspecting Key Components of the Exhaust System

A malfunctioning exhaust system can lead to dangerous situations, such as the infiltration of harmful fumes into the cab or sleeper berth.

Therefore, it is crucial to thoroughly examine key components of the exhaust system. Ensure that there are no loose, damaged, or missing exhaust pipes, tailpipes, mufflers, or vertical stacks. Additionally, verify that there are no leaks in the system.

Checking Emergency Equipment

Every vehicle should be equipped with emergency gear. This includes at least one functional, rated fire extinguisher. The vehicle should also have a warning system, which could consist of three liquid-burning flares or six regular flares, or three reflective warning triangles. It is also advisable to have spare electric fuses on hand.

Cargo Management (Trucks)

As a driver, it is your duty to ensure that the vehicle is not overloaded and that the cargo is evenly distributed and secured before embarking on a trip. If you are transporting hazardous materials, ensure you have all the necessary documentation and placards.

Mid-Trip Inspection

During the journey, pay close attention to the following items:

• Instrument panel

• Mirrors

• Temperature gauges

• Lights

• Tire pressure gauges

• Air pressure gauge

- Ammeter/voltmeter

- Cargo

- Cargo cover

Stay alert to the vehicle's performance while driving. If you notice an unusual smell or if the vehicle is not handling as expected, investigate the issue. Also, ensure all gauges are within their normal operating range.

Truck drivers and operators of truck tractors should inspect cargo security within the first 50 miles of the journey, and then every 150 miles or every three hours for the remainder of the trip.

Chapter 9: Basic Control

The ability to safely operate a vehicle largely depends on the effective control of its speed and direction. This requires proficiency in steering, acceleration, and braking.

Acceleration

When starting your vehicle, ensure it does not roll back as this could result in a collision with the vehicle behind you. To prevent this in a manual transmission vehicle, partially engage the clutch before removing your foot from the brake.

Safe Reversing

Reversing a commercial vehicle is a challenging task that demands extra caution from the driver. To ensure a safe and successful reversing process, begin in the correct position. The vehicle should be positioned optimally to facilitate a safe procedure, which will vary based on the reversing method of the vehicle.

Before moving backward, thoroughly inspect your path or travel line. For the best perspective, exit the vehicle and walk around it. Check the path on the sides and overhead, as well as in and near the path the vehicle will take.

Regularly check the mirrors on both sides of the vehicle. If you have any doubts, exit the vehicle and inspect the path again.

Reverse as slowly as possible, using the lowest reverse gear. This allows for quick correction of steering errors and enables you to stop promptly if necessary.

If possible, seek assistance. An additional person can help you navigate blind spots. Ask them to stand near the rear of the vehicle where you can see them.

Qualities of a Safe Driver

A competent driver is knowledgeable about their vehicle. You should be aware of your vehicle's positioning on the road and anticipate unexpected actions from other drivers. It's important to look ahead, but many drivers fail to realize they need to look even further ahead than they would in a car. Changing lanes may require a significant distance, which means you need to be aware of your surroundings at all times.

Just as looking ahead is crucial, it's equally important to be aware of what's happening behind and to the sides of your vehicle. Regularly check your mirrors, especially in heavy traffic or unusual situations.

In traffic, it's vital to check the mirrors on both sides and at the rear. This is crucial for sudden lane changes and to spot vehicles attempting to overtake you.

Be mindful that mirrors have inherent blind spots, areas that cannot be seen through the mirrors.

In certain traffic situations, more than just frequent mirror checks may be required. These situations include lane changes, merges, turns, and tight maneuvers. Each scenario requires a brief explanation.

Lane Transitions

Before switching lanes, it's crucial to check your mirrors to ensure there's no vehicle next to you or attempting to overtake you.

When to check your mirrors:

• Prior to changing lanes. It's important to verify that there's sufficient space.

• After activating your turn signal. Also, ensure that no vehicle has entered your blind spot.

• Right after initiating the lane change. Confirm that the path is clear.

• Upon completing the lane change.

• During merges.

• When merging into traffic, use your mirrors to ensure there's a sizable gap for you to enter safely.

• In tight maneuvers.

• When navigating through tight spaces or close quarters, always use your mirrors to ensure you have enough clearance.

Interacting with Other Motorists

Effective communication with other drivers is not only courteous but also vital for a safe journey. Always signal your intentions to allow other drivers time to respond.

Here are some general rules for signaling:

Turns

There are three fundamental rules for using turn signals.

Firstly, signal early to dissuade any other vehicle from attempting to overtake you.

Secondly, keep signaling. As both your hands are on the steering wheel during the turn, you shouldn't switch off the signal until the turn is successfully completed.

Lastly, cancel your signal. After completing the turn, remember to switch off the signal (unless your vehicle has self-canceling signals).

Indicate your vehicle is decelerating

Inform the vehicles behind you when you're about to slow down. This can be done by lightly tapping the brake pedal several times to flash the brake lights. If you're driving slowly, you can also alert other drivers by turning on the four-way emergency flashers.

Additionally, alert other vehicles in the following situations:

Obstacles ahead

Due to the size of your vehicle, other drivers may struggle to see around it and spot potential hazards ahead. Flash your brake lights to warn them of any situation that requires you to slow down.

Sharp turns

Many drivers underestimate how slowly a commercial vehicle needs to navigate sharp turns. Signal to the drivers behind you by braking early and decelerating your vehicle in a steady, gradual manner.

Slow driving

It's surprising how many drivers fail to realize how quickly they're approaching a slow-moving vehicle. If you need to drive slowly, warn the drivers behind you by activating your emergency flashers (where it's legal).

State laws differ on this matter, so be aware of the regulations in the state you're driving.

Avoid directing traffic. Some drivers may signal for a vehicle to overtake them when they believe it's safe. Avoid this behavior as it could easily result in an accident, potentially making you liable. The potential fines could cost you thousands of dollars, making it an unnecessary risk.

Driving in Low Visibility Conditions

It's unavoidable that you may have to operate a commercial vehicle under unfavorable weather conditions or during times of the day when visibility is compromised, such as at dawn or dusk. These are crucial moments when you need to ensure that your vehicle is visible to other drivers. If you're having trouble seeing other vehicles clearly, it's safe to assume that they may also be struggling to see you.

During such times, it's advisable to turn on your vehicle's lights. This includes not only your headlights but also your identification or clearance lights. Ensure your headlights are set to low beam to avoid causing discomfort to other drivers.

Roadside Parking

When parking your vehicle on the roadside, it's important to activate your four-way emergency lights, especially during the night. Relying solely on taillights may not provide adequate warning to other drivers. There have been instances where drivers have collided with the rear of parked trucks, mistaking them for moving vehicles.

Hazards

A risk on the road is a situation that presents potential danger. While we often associate risks with road conditions, they can also involve other road users such as drivers, pedestrians, or cyclists.

For instance, the vehicle ahead of you can become a risk if it suddenly decelerates while approaching a freeway exit.

Identifying risks before they escalate into emergencies allows you more time to react and prevent accidents. If a car abruptly swerves into your lane, early recognition of this action can give you enough time to switch lanes or slow down, check your mirrors, and signal your intentions.

Being vigilant can significantly reduce danger. If a driver fails to identify a risk until it's directly in front of them, it may be too late to prevent an accident. They might have to brake suddenly or swerve, both of which increase the likelihood of an accident.

Recognizing risks is a skill that can be learned. Usually, there are signs that a situation could escalate into a risk. While experience helps in identifying these signs, some can be recognized from your first day of driving.

If you encounter any of the following road conditions, you should reduce your speed and proceed with caution:

Obstacles on the Road

Any object on the road should be considered a risk. These can damage your vehicle's tires, rims, brakes, and electrical lines. Some objects may even get lodged between dual tires.

Some seemingly harmless objects can pose a threat. For example, a cardboard box might appear empty but could contain heavy or solid material. Paper and cloth bags are other examples of objects that may not be immediately recognized as dangerous.

You should learn to identify such potential risks early enough to avoid sudden braking or abrupt lane changes.

Exit and Entrance Ramps

An exit that sharply descends and requires a turn can be a risk. Vehicles naturally accelerate when going downhill, making it challenging to slow down and maintain a safe speed. The combination of braking and turning can further increase the risk.

To mitigate this risk, ensure you slow down before reaching the curved part of the exit or entrance ramp.

Distractions

Distracted individuals pose risks, and you should pay extra attention to them. Observe their focus and prepare for unexpected actions, even if they seem to have noticed you.

Children

Children may run across the road without checking for traffic, especially when chasing a toy. If children are nearby, slow down. If a ball rolls across the road, anticipate that a child might follow it.

Ice Cream Trucks

Children are often drawn to ice cream trucks. If you see one parked by the road, expect children to be around and slow down.

Engaged Individuals

Pay special attention to pedestrians or drivers engaged in conversation. Their attention is divided, and they may not be as alert to traffic.

Road Workers

Road workers can be risks as their presence can distract drivers. They might not notice approaching vehicles, so you should be vigilant.

Disabled Vehicles

A vehicle with its hood up or a jack underneath is a potential risk. Drivers fixing their vehicles may not be fully aware of the traffic, requiring you to be extra cautious.

Accidents

Accidents are obvious risks. Those involved may not be monitoring the traffic, and other drivers might be distracted by the scene, creating additional risks. Be prepared to slow down or stop suddenly when approaching an accident scene.

Confused Drivers

Drivers unfamiliar with the area can be risks. They might change lanes abruptly or stop unexpectedly. Signs of confusion include frequent braking, slow driving, or stopping mid-intersection.

Slow Drivers

Drivers moving slower than the average speed are risks. Identifying such vehicles from a distance can help you avoid a collision.

Turning Vehicles

Drivers planning to turn might slow down or stop, waiting for traffic or pedestrians to clear. Pay close attention to their indicators and be aware of the traffic they're dealing with.

Speed Considerations

Speed plays a significant role in numerous fatal accidents. It's crucial not only to adhere to the speed limit but also to modify your driving behavior according to the road conditions. This doesn't only apply to slowing down in adverse weather or poor visibility, but also adjusting your speed to accommodate increased traffic, curves, and hills.

There's a formula that aids drivers in comprehending the factors that contribute to a commercial vehicle's actual braking distance:

Perception Distance + Reaction Distance + Braking Distance = Total Stopping Distance

Perception distance refers to the distance the vehicle covers from the moment your eyes spot a hazard until your brain acknowledges it. For an alert driver, the perception time is roughly ¾ of a second. If the vehicle is moving at a speed of 55 mph, it covers approximately 81 feet per second in this ¾ of a second.

Braking distance is the distance covered from the moment you apply the brakes until the vehicle comes to a complete halt. Under optimal conditions—with good brakes and dry pavement—a commercial vehicle typically requires about 170 feet to stop within 4 ½ seconds.

Total stopping distance is the overall distance a vehicle requires to come to a complete stop. If the vehicle is moving at 55 mph, it typically takes around 6 seconds and 290 feet to stop completely. If the vehicle is moving at a higher speed, the stopping distance increases. In fact, every time the speed doubles, the vehicle requires four times the distance to stop. This implies that the vehicle possesses four times the destructive power in the event of a collision with another vehicle.

While a vehicle's stopping distance significantly increases at higher speeds, even a slight reduction in speed can substantially decrease the braking time.

The weight of a vehicle also affects the stopping distance. The heavier the vehicle, the more work the brakes have to do when it stops, causing them to absorb more heat. Components such as brakes, springs, tires, and even shock absorbers are designed to be most effective when the vehicle is fully loaded.

It's important to remember that an empty truck has less traction than one carrying cargo, and therefore requires a greater stopping distance.

Practices for Ensuring Safe Driving

Avoid driving when you're distracted. This behavior endangers not only your life but also the lives of other road users and your passengers. Engaging in any other activity while driving constitutes distracted driving. Any action that diverts your full attention from the road is a distraction.

If you're not focusing on the road or if you're removing your hands from the steering wheel, you're engaging in distracted driving.

Distracted driving isn't limited to physical distractions. Any mental activity that diverts your attention from your driving duties is also considered a distraction. If your mind is preoccupied with other thoughts, even if you're looking at the road, you're still distracted.

There are guidelines to help you prevent distracted driving. Some of the most effective ones include:

• Familiarize yourself with all the features of your vehicle, including safety features and electronic devices, before you start driving.

• Load your favorite music CDs or other music formats before you hit the road. Only change them at rest stops or truck stops, not while driving.

• Pre-set your preferred radio stations.

- Remove any unnecessary objects from the vehicle.

- Adjust all mirrors for optimal visibility before you start your journey.

- Plan your route in advance, including any necessary permits.

- Avoid reading or writing while driving.

- Refrain from engaging in intense or emotional conversations with passengers.

- Do not smoke, eat, or drink while driving.

- If possible, switch off your cell phone while driving.

- If you can't switch it off, avoid making or receiving calls while driving. If it's an urgent call, find a safe place to pull over.

- Even though some states allow hands-free devices, be aware that using these can still cause distractions.

- If you must use your cell phone while driving, keep the conversation brief. Never engage in lengthy, casual conversations while driving.

• Avoid using your phone in areas with heavy vehicle or pedestrian traffic, road construction, or adverse weather conditions.

• Refrain from texting or reading texts or other messages while driving.

Be Vigilant of Distracted Drivers

It's crucial to be aware of other drivers who may be distracted, as they pose a potential risk on the road. Identifying signs of distracted driving can help you react promptly and prevent accidents. Indicators of distracted driving may include:

• Veering within or beyond their lane.

• Varying speeds inconsistently.

• Engaging in conversation with passengers.

• Using a mobile phone, eating, or performing any activity that diverts attention from driving.

When you spot such drivers, maintain a safe distance. If you need to overtake a distracted driver, proceed with caution, as they may not be aware of your approach.

Handling Aggressive Drivers and Road Rage

Road rage, though not a new issue, is becoming more common due to increasing traffic congestion. It is characterized by intense anger, often violent, triggered by the stress and frustration experienced by drivers in challenging situations.

Aggressive driving refers to any deliberate behavior by a driver that endangers people or property. This can range from risky maneuvers to outright violence. Common aggressive driving behaviors include speeding, tailgating, weaving through traffic, overtaking on the shoulder, obstructing traffic, honking and shouting, flashing headlights, and making offensive gestures. Extreme instances of aggressive driving may involve ramming into a vehicle or brandishing a weapon.

Given the potential damage your vehicle can cause, it's crucial to avoid aggressive driving. Your mindset before you even start the car plays a significant role in how you handle driving stress.

Here are some strategies to help you stay calm during your journey:

• Listen to soothing music or any tunes that help you relax.

• Concentrate on driving and avoid distractions.

• Be realistic about travel times. Account for potential delays like traffic, adverse weather, or roadworks when planning your arrival time.

• If you're running late, accept it and avoid getting agitated.

• Be understanding towards other drivers. Try to empathize with why they might be driving poorly.

• Reduce your speed and keep a safe distance from the vehicle ahead.

Etiquette in the Left Lane

Nothing seems to incite more fury on the road than a vehicle moving slower than the surrounding traffic in the left lane. If you encounter such a vehicle, refrain from making any inappropriate gestures, even seemingly harmless ones like shaking your head.

Always remember to exercise caution and courtesy while driving; if another driver wishes to overtake you, don't accelerate to block them. Allow them to pass.

Dealing with Aggressive Drivers

Aggressive driving is characterized by any on-road behavior that deliberately endangers another person or property, with a blatant disregard for safety. The severity of aggressive driving can range from risky maneuvers to extreme violence.

Typical aggressive driving behaviors include tailgating, erratic lane changes, overtaking on the shoulder, speeding, obstructing traffic, honking excessively, shouting, flashing headlights, and making obscene gestures. In extreme cases, it can escalate to physical contact with another vehicle or even brandishing weapons.

If you encounter an aggressive driver attempting to provoke you into reckless driving, do everything in your power to increase the distance between your vehicles and move out of their way. Do not engage in any challenge that involves speeding.

It's advisable to ignore their gestures and avoid reacting to them. It's even wise to avoid making eye contact.

If you believe their driving poses a threat to public safety, report them to the relevant authorities. Provide the police or highway patrol with a description of the vehicle, its location, license plate number, and the direction it's heading.

Night Driving

Driving in the dark is significantly riskier than daytime driving due to the increased difficulty in identifying hazards, giving you less time to respond. The challenges of night driving are linked to the driver, the vehicle, and the road conditions.

One of the main issues for the driver is impaired vision. Many people's visual acuity decreases at night. This is partly because the human eye requires time to adapt to low light conditions.

The dazzling effect of bright lights can momentarily impair a driver's vision, with older individuals being especially susceptible. It may take up to two seconds to recover from such glare. While this may not seem like a significant amount of time, a vehicle moving at 55 mph can cover 150 feet in that duration.

To mitigate this risk, avoid staring directly into bright lights while driving. Instead, focus on the right side of the road, and when an oncoming vehicle approaches, shift your gaze to the sidelines.

Driving while tired at night is a serious hazard. Many people struggle to stay awake and alert, particularly after midnight. If you feel drowsy or fatigued, it's crucial to pull over as soon as it's safe and rest. Continuing to drive in such a state endangers not only your life but also the lives of others.

Road conditions that make night driving more challenging include inadequate lighting. While some areas have bright streetlights, most night driving is done with limited additional lighting, relying primarily on the vehicle's headlights.

The lack of light makes it harder to spot hazards as quickly as during the day. Roads without lights make it challenging to spot cars, pedestrians, cyclists, and animals. Even well-lit roads can pose dangers, as neon signs and other lights can obscure traffic signals and road signs.

Whether it's nighttime or poor lighting, it's crucial to reduce your speed to ensure you have enough time to stop if a hazard appears.

At night, your vehicle's headlights often provide the only illumination, enabling you to see the road and other drivers. Low beams typically illuminate approximately 250 feet ahead, while high beams extend visibility to between 300 and 500 feet. Given these distances, you should adjust your speed to ensure your stopping distance is well within your sight range.

Dirty headlights can cut your visibility distance by half, further impairing your night vision and making it harder for other drivers to see your vehicle. Before embarking on a journey, ensure your headlights are clean and functioning correctly.

Also, check that the headlights are properly aligned and not pointing in the wrong direction. Misaligned headlights can not only reduce your visibility but may also dazzle other drivers.

Utilizing Additional Lights

To ensure your visibility to other drivers, it's imperative to ascertain that all the following lights are clean and functioning correctly:

- Clearance lights

- Marker lights

- Identification lights

- Taillights

- Reflectors

Brake lights and turn signals are particularly vital for your safety and that of other drivers during nighttime. Before embarking on your journey, ensure these are clean and working correctly.

Mirrors and Windshields

A dirty mirror or windshield can create a glare at night, potentially impairing your vision. This becomes particularly problematic when driving towards the sun. Even a seemingly clean windshield can reveal dirt when faced with direct sunlight. Regularly cleaning both the inside and outside of your windshield is a recommended habit.

Avoid Blinding Other Drivers

The glare from your vehicle's headlights can cause visibility issues for oncoming drivers, especially when the lights reflect off the rearview mirrors of drivers in front of you. Ensure your high beams are not on during these instances.

Avoiding Glare from Other Vehicles

To prevent being blinded by oncoming vehicles, avoid looking directly into their lights. Instead, shift your gaze slightly towards the right lane or the right edge marking. If oncoming drivers have their high beams on, do not reciprocate. This only increases the likelihood of blinding the other driver and potentially causing an accident.

Feel free to use high beams when alone on the highway for better road visibility. However, refrain from using high beam headlights when within 500 feet of an oncoming vehicle.

Maintain a dimly lit cab interior. Excessive brightness inside can compromise your ability to see the road. Turn off interior lights and keep the instrument panel lights on a low setting.

Driving in Fog

If possible, avoid driving in foggy conditions. If you encounter fog while driving, it's safer to pull over at a truck stop and wait for improved visibility. However, if driving in fog is unavoidable, adhere to the following guidelines:

• Pay attention to all fog-related warning signs

• Slow down before entering a foggy area

• Activate your four-way flashers to increase your visibility to other vehicles

• Use fog lights and low-beam headlights, even in daytime fog

• Stay vigilant for other drivers who may not have their lights on

Remember, the taillights of the vehicle ahead may not accurately indicate the road's position as the vehicle could be off the road. Instead, use roadside reflectors to guide you and determine the road's curvature ahead.

Listen for unseen traffic and be cautious of vehicles on the side of the road. Unless absolutely necessary, avoid pulling over to the side of the road and refrain from overtaking other vehicles.

Driving Around Bars and Clubs

It's crucial to remain vigilant when driving around the closing hours of bars, taverns, and clubs. There's a high probability that many departing patrons may have consumed enough alcohol to hinder their driving abilities.

Keep an eye out for drivers who halt without cause or struggle to maintain their lane. These behaviors could suggest that they are under the influence of alcohol or drugs.

Winter Driving

Winter driving can pose significant risks. Prior to driving in the winter months, perform a routine pre-trip inspection with a particular focus on the following areas:

Windshield Wipers and Washer Fluid

Ensure that the wiper blades are functioning correctly and exert enough pressure against the windshield to clean it effectively. If they fail to do so, they may not remove snow efficiently, compromising your visibility.

Ensure that the windshield fluid reservoir is full and operational. Also, ensure you have washer fluid antifreeze to prevent freezing.

If your windshield wipers are not providing a clear view, stop and address the issue as soon as it is safe to do so.

Tires

Maintaining sufficient tire tread is crucial for safe winter driving. Your vehicle requires adequate traction to navigate through snow. The steering tires must have sufficient tread to safely turn corners and navigate curves.

What constitutes sufficient tread?

Each major groove on the front tires should have a tread depth of 4/32-inch. All other tires should have a minimum tread depth of 2/32-inch. Use a gauge to ensure your tires are winter-ready.

Tire Chains

In certain weather conditions, driving without tire chains may be impossible. Hence, always carry an appropriate number of chains and extra cross-links to fit your vehicle's tires. Regularly inspect the chains to ensure there are no broken cross-links, hooks, or side chains.

It's advisable to familiarize yourself with the process of installing the chains before you actually need them.

Slippery Surfaces

When faced with slippery roads, pull over as soon as it is safe to do so. If you must drive under such conditions, start off gently and slowly, focusing on understanding the road conditions.

Ice?

Be prepared for icy conditions on bridges and overpasses while driving. If other vehicles aren't spraying debris, it's a sign that ice has formed. You can also identify icy conditions by checking for ice on the mirrors and wiper blades. If there's ice, it's likely that the road is icy too.

Adjust Braking and Turning to Fit Conditions

Avoid using the engine brake or speed retarder in harsh winter conditions as it can cause the vehicle to skid on slippery roads. Always adapt your speed to these conditions. Don't rely solely on posted speed limit signs, as they are designed for ideal weather conditions.

Maintain a steady speed to avoid sudden braking or acceleration.

Avoid applying the brake while taking curves and approach them more slowly in winter conditions.

Remember, as the weather warms and ice begins to melt, the road can become increasingly slippery and hazardous.

Driving in High Temperatures

During the sweltering summer season, it's crucial to conduct your regular pre-trip inspection, but with particular attention to certain areas.

Tires

It's essential to thoroughly inspect the tire mounting and air pressure. In extremely hot weather, tires should be checked every 100 miles or every two hours. Air pressure tends to increase in high temperatures. Avoid releasing air as when the weather cools down, the tire pressure will be insufficient.

If the tire is too hot to touch, cease driving until it cools down to prevent potential blowouts or fires.

Engine Oil

Engine oil serves to lubricate the engine, but it also aids in cooling it down. During your pre-trip inspection, ensure that there is sufficient engine oil. While driving, regularly monitor the oil temperature gauge to ensure it remains within the appropriate range.

Engine Coolant

Ensure that the engine cooling system has an adequate amount of water and antifreeze during your pre-trip inspection. Refer to the manufacturer's manual for the correct quantities. Antifreeze is crucial in both hot and cold weather.

Avoid opening the radiator cap unless it's cool enough to touch with your bare hand. Follow these steps when adding coolant:

1. Switch off the engine.

2. Allow the engine to cool down.

3. Using gloves or a thick cloth, gently turn the radiator cap to the first stop to release the pressure seal.

4. Step back while the pressure is being released.

5. Once the pressure has been released, push down on the cap and turn it further to remove it.

6. Check the coolant level and add more if necessary.

7. Replace the cap and ensure it's securely closed.

Engine Belts

In extremely hot weather, the tar on the road can rise to the surface, making it slippery.

Drive at a moderate speed to avoid overheating in hot weather. High-speed driving only increases heat on the tires and engine. Inspect belts for cracks or other signs of wear.

Hoses

Ensure that the coolant hoses are in good condition. A ruptured coolant hose can not only lead to engine failure but also potentially cause a fire.

Chapter 10: Practice Test

1. How much chlorine must you be transporting to necessitate stopping at a railroad crossing?

a) Over 3 ounces

b) Over 3 pounds

c) Over 12 pounds

d) Any quantity

Answer: d) Any quantity

If your vehicle, marked with a hazard sign, is carrying any quantity of chlorine or if you are operating a tank vehicle used for transporting hazardous materials, you are obligated to halt the vehicle 15 to 50 feet before the closest rail before proceeding to cross.

2. Which of the following substances cannot be classified with a hazard category or identification number?

a) Poison

b) Oxygen

c) Non-hazardous substance

d) Explosives

Answer: c) Non-hazardous substance

Only hazardous substances are permitted to be categorized with a hazard class or assigned an identification number.

3. The transport index of radioactive cargo provides information about _____.

a) The level of caution required during transportation

b) The price of the substance

c) The manufacturer of the substance

d) The weight of the cargo

Answer: a) The level of caution required during transportation

Radioactive cargo can emit radiation affecting nearby packages, thus necessitating careful handling during shipment. The transport index provides information about the level of caution required.

4. Hazardous materials are characterized as _____.

a) Items that obstruct the driver's field of vision while driving.

b) Substances that pose a potential risk to public safety during transportation.

c) Substances that are intended to be discarded.

d) Items that limit the full maneuverability of the vehicle.

Answer: b) Substances that pose a potential risk to public safety during transportation.

5. Which of the following statements is accurate according to the Hazardous Materials Regulations?

a) A commercial driver must have a college degree to transport hazardous materials.

b) All commercial vehicles transporting hazardous materials must display appropriate warning signs.

c) No vehicle carrying hazardous materials should travel on any highway.

d) All of the above

Answer: b) All commercial vehicles transporting hazardous materials must display appropriate warning signs.

6. What should students do when they board the bus?

a) Occupy the back row first.

b) Fill the back row only when all other seats are occupied.

c) Sit as far away from the driver as possible.

d) Sit next to their best friend to minimize disturbances.

Answer: b) Fill the back row only when all other seats are occupied.

Students should only resort to sitting in the back row of the bus when all other seats are occupied. Sitting closer to the front of the bus is safer, especially in the event of a rear-end collision. Students with special needs should always be seated near the driver for their convenience and safety.

7. When should you activate the right-side indicator before pulling over?

a) 3 to 5 seconds.

b) 10 to 15 seconds.

c) 15 to 25 seconds.

d) 1 to 3 seconds.

Answer: a) 3 to 5 seconds.

It's essential never to pull the school bus over without activating the right indicator. You should turn it on 3 to 5 seconds before pulling over to allow other drivers behind you to react accordingly.

8. What should a student do if they drop an item while approaching the school bus?

a) Immediately stop and pick it up.

b) Request another student to pick it up for them.

c) Ask the driver to pick it up.

d) Leave it and purchase a replacement.

Answer: c) Ask the driver to pick it up.

A student should never attempt to pick up a dropped item. This could put them out of the driver's sight, creating a potentially hazardous situation. Instead, they should move away from the bus's danger zones, inform the driver, and let the driver retrieve the item.

9. Which mirror provides a view of the back tires at the point where they touch the ground?

a) The external flat mirrors.

b) The external convex mirrors.

c) The external crossover mirrors.

d) The internal rearview mirrors.

Answer: a) The external flat mirrors.

The correct adjustment of the external flat mirrors ensures a clear view of approximately 200 feet—about the length of four buses—from behind, the sides of the bus, and the back tires where they touch the ground.

10. Which statement is incorrect about external convex mirrors?

a) They do not provide an accurate distance or size of objects.

b) They assist in viewing the students on the bus.

c) They reflect the accurate size of people.

d) They provide a broad view of the bus's exterior.

Answer: c) They reflect the accurate size of people.

These mirrors offer a panoramic view of the bus's exterior on both the left and right sides. While they allow you to see students on the side of the bus, traffic, and other activities, they do not accurately reflect the size of individuals.

11. What should be done with the parking brake when the vehicle is left unattended?

a) It should always be engaged

b) It should only be engaged if the vehicle is parked on a slope

c) It should not be engaged as it could damage the tires

d) None of the above

Answer: a) It should always be engaged

As a rule of thumb, always engage the parking brake when you park your vehicle. The only exceptions to this rule are when the brakes are extremely hot or if they are wet and the temperature is below freezing.

12. What is the role of an air compressor in the air brake system?

a) To pump air into the air storage tanks

b) To inflate the tires

c) To direct the air to the rear of the truck

d) To direct the air to the front of the truck

Answer: a) To pump air into the air storage tanks

The air brake system includes a compressor, which is regulated by a governor, that pumps air into the storage tanks.

13. If the vehicle has dual parking control valves, a separate air tank can be used to _____.

a) Temporarily disengage the spring brakes

b) Enhance the efficiency of the air brakes

c) Adjust the brakes on the rear of the trailer

d) None of the above

Answer: a) Temporarily disengage the spring brakes

Dual parking control valves come with a separate tank that can be used to disengage the spring brakes if needed. This may be necessary if the air pressure drops too low. They are only activated for a brief period, allowing you to move the vehicle in case of an emergency.

14. What is used to operate the brakes?

a) Compressed air

b) Ambient air

c) Non-compressed air

d) None of the above

Answer: a) Compressed air

Many commercial vehicles are equipped with air brakes that utilize compressed air to operate.

15. At what pressure should the low air pressure warning signal activate?

a) 120 psi

b) 15 psi

c) 100 psi

d) 60 psi

Answer: d) 60 psi

A low air pressure warning signal should be triggered when the air pressure in the tanks drops below 60 psi. The warning can be indicated in one of three ways: a light, a buzzer, or a wigwag.

16. The _____ is responsible for maintaining the air pressure in the air brake system.

a) air compressor

b) water pump

c) alternator

d) power steering

Answer: a) air compressor

The air compressor is tasked with pumping air into the air storage tanks to sustain the air pressure required for the air brakes. If the compressor operates via a belt-driven mechanism, it's crucial to ensure the belt is tightly fitted. A loose belt could potentially slip, compromising the efficiency of the air compressor.

17. The _____ should be free from dirt, unauthorized stickers, obstructions, or any form of damage.

a) lighting indicators

b) headlights

c) windshield and mirrors

d) none of the above

Answer: c) windshield and mirrors

During the pre-trip inspection, it's essential to ensure that the windshields and mirrors are clean and undamaged. They should be devoid of any unauthorized stickers or objects that could obstruct your view.

18. Engine compartment belts should not exhibit more than ____.

a) up to three-quarters inch play at the center of the belt

b) up to three-quarters inch play at the ends of the belt

c) up to one-half inch play at the center of the belt

d) no play is allowed

Answer: a) up to three-quarters inch play at the center of the belt

In the course of the pre-trip inspection, it's necessary to verify that the following belts: power steering, water pump, alternator, and air compressor, are tightly fitted and exhibit no more than three-quarters inch play at the center of the belts.

19. Which of the following is not required to be checked in the engine compartment during a pre-trip inspection?

a) oil level

b) oil pressure

c) power steering fluid

d) coolant

Answer: b) oil pressure

During the pre-trip inspection, it's mandatory to inspect the engine compartment for leaks, and check the levels of oil, coolant, and power steering fluid. However, checking the oil pressure is not required.

20. When checking the coolant level:

a) Do not remove the radiator cap unless the truck is running and up to operating temperature

b) Remove the radiator cap if the engine is not hot or inspect the reservoir sight glass

c) Ensure you're wearing safety glasses and rubber gloves

d) None of the above

Answer: b) Remove the radiator cap if the engine is not hot or inspect the reservoir sight glass

It's critical to remember not to remove the radiator cap if the engine is running or still hot.

Conclusion

We sincerely appreciate your faith in us, entrusting us with your aspiration to acquire a Commercial Driver's License (CDL). Given the plethora of test preparation and study resources available today, we are honored that you have selected us to guide you through this significant phase of your professional journey.

This book was meticulously crafted with the highest regard for accuracy, comprehensiveness, and factual information, aimed at helping you ace your commercial driver's license exam on your first attempt. Pursuing a professional driving career is a rewarding choice, offering the opportunity to traverse the highways and routes of North America. The chance to explore the nation's roads and witness its breathtaking beauty is truly unparalleled!

We hope that the information provided in this book has shed light on the regulations, standards, and precedents governing the automotive and transportation sectors. These rules have been painstakingly devised and implemented by experts who have conducted extensive research to ensure the safest and most efficient means of travel on our nation's highways.

For more in-depth information directly from the authorities, we encourage you to visit the websites of the federal agencies mentioned in this book, including the Transportation Security Administration (TSA), the Professional Truck Driver Institute (PDTI), the Department of Transportation (DOT), among others.

Once again, we extend our heartfelt thanks for your readership and wish you the very best in your examinations and your forthcoming career as a commercial driver!

Made in the USA
Columbia, SC
14 July 2024

38612794R00096